The Form Tutor:

New Approaches To
Tutoring For The 1990s

WITHDRAWN

Blackwell Studies in Personal and Social Education and Pastoral Care

Edited by Peter Lang and Peter Ribbins

The Form Tutor:
New Approaches To
Tutoring For The 1990s

Philip Griffiths
and
Keith Sherman

BLACKWELL EDUCATION

First published 1991

Published by
Basil Blackwell Ltd
108 Cowley Road
Oxford OX4 1JF

British Library Cataloguing in Publication Data
Griffiths, Philip
The form tutor: new approaches to tutoring in the 1990s.
– (Blackwell studies in personal and social education and
pastoral care)
1. Great Britain. Secondary schools. Teaching
I. Title   II. Sherman, Keith
373.13028140941

ISBN 0–631–16124–4
ISBN 0–631–15663–1 pbk

We should like to offer our thanks to the Dudley Education Authority for permission to conduct our research; to the Heads, Deputies and 'Pastoral Managers' who bore with our questioning and who shared with us ideas, concerns, plans, strategies and hopes; but above all to the 'heroes' of this book, the teachers involved in tutoring who answered our questionnaires, talked with us at length, confirmed our impressions and fulfilled our expectations.

This book is dedicated to Barbara and Carol: for patience over and above the call of duty.

Typeset in 10/12 pt Plantin Roman
by Graphicraft Typesetters Ltd., Hong Kong
Printed by T.J. Press (Padstow) Ltd, Cornwall

Contents

Foreword

For more than a decade the claim that the tutor's role is central to their pastoral care has been made by innumerable secondary schools. Equally the idea of the tutor being the front line of the school's pastoral activities has been a notion glibly included in school prospectuses and embedded in the rhetoric of introductory parents' evenings. However, for just as long researchers, administrators and practitioners have been aware of how hollow many of these claims have been, in reality tutors often being bypassed or ignored when it comes to important decisions, many feeling themselves untrained, unsupported and inadequate. Few schools have managed to give their tutors real responsibility for their tutees or the support and time they need to take it.

A limited number of books have been written on the work of the tutor, and at least some of these have tended to ignore many of the real issues and problems that surround it. Thus any competent new text on the area should be welcome. With the 1990s we are entering a new era so far as education is concerned, and many of the ideas that related to effective tutoring in the 1980s are now out of date. In the light of this, this book is especially welcome for not only does it confront some of the real issues of tutoring, it also provides a new and innovatory perspective appropriate to the new decade. This book is intended to challenge but also to provide the reader with the ideas and information needed to respond to that challenge. It is a very welcome and timely addition to the literature of an area which is likely to increase in importance in the immediate future.

Peter Lang

1
Introduction

It has been possible, over the last few years, to see the beginnings of a significant change in the way schools tackle the job of looking after and developing the 'whole person' of their students: a change of magnitude equivalent to that which created the pastoral positions of Heads of Year and House, or Heads of Upper and Lower Schools, some 20 to 25 years ago. A variety of factors, ranging from discontent with existing structures and anxiety about the pastoral/academic divide, to the emphasis now placed on individual pupils taking greater responsibility for their own learning, have together fuelled a movement which is increasing the breadth and importance of the tutor's role and placing the tutor and the process of tutoring closer to the centre of the school's activities.

Major characteristics of that movement, which can be observed in schools up and down the country, are

- the development of the co-ordinating function of the tutor, monitoring each pupil's overall progress and negotiating profiles of achievement;
- the development of the advocate role – the 'pupil's mentor, agent and protector of her interests against the system' as the Head of Knowle High School, Blackpool described it (*Times Educational Supplement*, 3rd February 1989);
- the development of the pupil support role, with responsibility for meeting parents, consulting educational welfare officers and educational psychologists, calling meetings of subject specialists who teach their pupils and, where necessary, negotiating timetabled behaviour modification targets and reviews.

The increasing importance of the tutor's role does not mean that Pastoral Managers, Heads of Year, Heads of House and so on are going to disappear, although they are likely to change their functions and perhaps their titles. The reasons for the creation of those management positions – whether

5

it was, as has been rather cynically suggested, to find jobs for non-academic secondary modern teachers or to break large schools into administratively viable units – seem to us now to be totally unimportant. The fact that the positions were created meant that for the first time school resources, ie time and money, were put into pastoral work. It was recognised as important and it was paid for. The result has been that over the past 20 years or so a degree of expertise in a range of skills has been developed, particularly by those in pastoral management positions, which did not exist before. Unfortunately, in most schools the very development of that expertise also meant that the pastoral managers took responsibility for the majority of 'pastoral work' themselves, with a consequent reduction in the authority and status of form tutors and the task of tutoring, and hence little opportunity for tutors to become equally skilled.

We believe the task for the 1990s, and the next step in what is essentially an evolutionary process, is for the balance to be restored, for pastoral expertise to be spread more widely and for the pastoral skills of tutors to be developed to match their increasingly important central role.

That will still leave a vital task for pastoral managers, although a necessarily different one. A developed tutorial role can only be sustained if it is matched by a parallel development in the 'pastoral care of staff', and the job of the pastoral manager will be to enable, 'manage' and support the work and person of the form tutor. It is our firm belief that an ethos of care in a school must encompass both staff and pupils, and that any school which does not care for its staff – in the widest professional sense – is unlikely to get the care of its pupils right. The induction, support, development and – even if informally – appraisal of its staff are therefore essential components of a school's system of pastoral care. The movement to look at the pupil as a whole person must be complemented by looking at the form tutor, or rather the teacher who for part of their time is also a form tutor, as a whole person: a whole person with pastoral needs rather than, as in most of the literature, a tool which the institution, through its middle management, uses to 'do a job' on the pupils.

This book is therefore only partly aimed at the tutor who wishes to analyse the processes underlying the tasks which face him or her, and to look for a few signposts to make sense of those tasks. It is aimed equally at the pastoral advisers and the senior tutors; the managers whose job it is to make the form tutors' job possible.

Throughout the book we have argued the need to recognise that the teacher as subject specialist, as well as the teacher as form tutor, contributes to the caring function of the school; that the pastoral/academic split is neither real nor necessary, since the roles of subject teacher and form tutor are both part of the unified role of the 'teacher' – a role which is concerned with the development of the whole child and which in the future could well be in all aspects essentially 'tutorial'. In fact the teacher in the future seems likely to need two areas of skill above all others:

1 the skill to guide and facilitate the learning of other individuals
2 the skill of promoting positive interaction in groups.

These two skills are clearly part of the pastoral repertoire but are equally necessary within the academic context. They belong to the teacher's and the pupil's whole experience in school.

If the academic/pastoral split is neither real nor necessary, then the idea of a 'pastoral curriculum', separate and distinct from the 'academic' one, is equally false and misleading. In its narrowest sense the term 'pastoral curriculum' is used to describe the content of the programmes followed by pupils, either with their tutors in that discrete timetable slot known as PSE (*Active Tutorial Work* is one of the best-known examples of this), or in specific 'social education' or 'health education' lessons outside the tutor period.

Whatever the content of such programmes – health or social education, citizenship or relationships – many other subjects on the timetable overlap in content and therefore must make a considerable contribution to a pupil's 'personal and social education'; a concept that will be reinforced by the emphasis being given to the cross-curricular themes of the National Curriculum. In a wider sense, therefore, the 'pastoral curriculum' can be seen as involving the content of most, perhaps all, subjects on the timetable.

But what distinguishes ATW and other tutorial programmes is not so much the content as the 'process': a process in which the tutor becomes a facilitator and the tutor group is encouraged to make decisions, to have some control over the content and to take an increasing responsibility for planning, implementation and outcomes, not just within the programme but in all aspects of the form's work – and indeed in all of their lives. This process demands of the tutor specific teaching strategies and skills:

● skills in handling individuals – not just in crisis situations but in regular reviews and conscious development
● skills in making and maintaining personal contact, in monitoring the progress, achievement and/or problems of each pupil; making each pupil feel valued and enhancing their self-image
● skills in handling groups, including handling controversial and sensitive issues, personal conflict and disaffection
● skills in administration and particularly in approaching necessary administrative tasks positively, in a way which allows them to become an essential part of the process through which clear messages are put across about security, status, stability, place etc.

There was a hope, behind the development of such programmes, that the skills and attitudes developed by being an effective form tutor would spill over into subject teaching, and increase the effectiveness of that teaching. This has always seemed to us similar to encouraging the tail to wag the dog;

to ignore the fact that many of the skills and strategies being recommended for use by form tutors had been developed within the academic curriculum over many years, particularly in subjects like English. These skills and strategies were the foundation for the successful introduction of GCSE and the development of Flexible Learning and the whole TVEI philosophy. The 'process' component of the 'academic' curriculum has always, therefore, made a significant contribution to the 'pastoral' curriculum.

If a significant part of the pastoral curriculum is how a pupil is treated in lesson time then we cannot ignore how the pupil is treated outside the classroom, within that whole area usually referred to as the 'hidden' curriculum. The messages about personal value and responsibility are just as strong from this as they are from the classroom experience, and must be planned just as carefully.

In its widest sense, therefore, if a school's curriculum is the plan of the learning experiences the school offers, then the 'pastoral' curriculum, aimed at developing not just knowledge and skills but confidence, responsibility and self-awareness, must encompass the whole of a pupil's experience in school, from the way in which she is given the results of a History test to the treatment she receives on a wet break-time; from his opportunity to contribute towards an Open Evening to the handling of his difficulty with Mathematics. In this sense the pastoral curriculum is the responsibility of all teachers, as subject specialists as well as form tutors.

We have difficulty in talking and writing about 'the form tutor'. Since in schools we tend to think in terms of ranks and titles, the words sound as if they describe a position, a person of a certain grade on a certain scale – or even a job to which someone has been appointed. Furthermore, as organisational charts make clear, 'form tutors' belong at the bottom of school hierarchies.

In fact, as we suggested earlier, the words 'form tutor' describe one function of the majority of the staff in any school – that of tutoring a group of children. Somehow, when the act of tutoring is turned into 'being a tutor' and is further translated into 'the form tutor', a process similar to reification takes place. An action, fluid, flexible, and transitive, expressing a relationship between two sorts of people, is turned into something concrete and intransitive, as if 'the form tutor' has an existence quite separate from the act and function of tutoring, or could go on being a form tutor even if there were no form to tutor.

So perhaps we need to get this quite clear from the start; that when we talk about 'the form tutor' we are talking about all teachers, or at least at any one time the majority, of teachers in any school, of various ranks and titles. All teachers are, have been, or will be, form tutors; and all tutors, for approximately the other 90 per cent of their working time, teach a subject. Tutors and subject teachers are not separate people; they do not have separate skills, personalities, experiences or ways of relating to pupils any more than the pupils themselves have separate personalities in the form room and the science lab. The way a teacher regards a pupil in the French or Physics lesson, talks to him, reprimands her, or praises her, will be the way that teacher/tutor talks to, reprimands or praises the 'tutee' in the 'form'. We are talking about one and the same person, who will carry into each context not only their skills but their values, their attitudes to pupils and their ways of speaking to them and relating to them. When we train form tutors we are also training teachers; when we talk about tutor skills we are talking about teaching skills.

Fundamental to the exercise of such skills, and indeed to all teaching and 'tutorial' work in it widest sense, is that much used and abused word the 'relationship' between the teacher/tutor and the pupil. A significant proportion of this book is spent on an attempt to clarify this central mystique and delineate not only the relationship but how it might be achieved in practical terms. We are aware that the reaction of many teachers to the word 'relationships' is similar to 'Whenever I hear the word "culture" . . . I reach for my gun'. We make no apology, however, for insisting on its central importance. As one subject teacher and form tutor said in his leaving speech to his colleagues in one of our schools, moved by the reaction of the pupils to the fact that he was going,

> 'That's what it's all about. That relationship between the teacher and the kids is everything – more important than your subject. Once you have the relationship then you can start to teach your subject. Without the relationship there's no point in trying to teach them anything.'

We would go as far as to say that a child's education is incomplete without the opportunity to experience at least one significant relationship with such a thinking and caring adult.

2
Prescriptions

At a recent workshop on 'The Role of the Form Tutor' a group of teachers were invited to consider a number of situations, amongst which were the following. They were asked to decide what action, if any, they thought was necessary or appropriate:

'The school demands a high degree of punctuality from its pupils, placing members of staff in strategic positions at 08.55 so as to catch the panting stragglers and administer suitable rebukes and punishments. Roy, a boy in your form, is continually in trouble for being late. After much trying, you get out of him the fact that Mother has left home, his Dad has to leave for work at 6 am and that he has to dress his little brother every morning and take him round to his Gran's for the day.'

'Jane is a member of your Year 10 form. She has a history of disruptive behaviour and suffers from a personal hygiene problem which makes her unpopular with both staff and other pupils, though you find her relatively easy to get on with. During an English lesson her teacher – the Head of Department and a woman who freely and loudly admits to disliking Jane – has spent a considerable amount of time attacking her for her appearance, smell and lack of work. Eventually Jane has turned on her and made a comment along the lines of "What about you – have you looked in the mirror recently?" The teacher's response to this is to scream "Don't you get personal with me, young lady" followed by a demand that Jane get out of the classroom. The teacher is now saying that she will not have Jane back but will not agree to her joining another set in her department.'

'From conversations with Lorraine, a 13-year-old girl in your tutor group, it becomes clear that she is regularly having sex with her 19-year-old boy friend.'

'A boy in your class has developed warts on his hands and two or three are appearing on his face. The boy seems unaware of them. He would like a job in a supermarket, but after a recent period of work experience in one, the manager has pointed out to the school that he could not be let near customers because of this problem. He will be going for job interviews in two or three months time. You have written to his parents suggesting that they contact their GP, but no action seems to have been taken.'

It might be thought legitimate to question which, if any, of those situations really belong within the frame of reference of a teacher's work and whether in fact a teacher/tutor has any right to do anything about any of them. Certainly, dealing with situations such as these is far removed from the job which, from outside, is normally seen as 'teaching': the delivery of information, or the development of skills, in a specific school subject. Yet no one at that conference felt that any of the exercises was extreme or even all that unusual in the daily life of a group of form tutors, and extended and sometimes heated discussion took place as individuals tried to work out what they would do in each situation. It became apparent that such situations do face form tutors; perhaps not continuously, perhaps not over such a wide range in the life of any one particular tutor, but certainly as part of the 'reality' of the job.

It is certainly legitimate to address the question (as we later will) of just what skills and experience a 'typical' form tutor has or would need to develop in order to grapple with such a 'reality'. Clearly a well-developed self-image, a good measure of confidence (even though that is difficult to define) and a 'knowledge of the world' would be an advantage, as would some awareness of counselling skills. Equally clearly, however, tutors will vary enormously in the degree that they have developed these, let alone the more specific 'skills' which we will be referring to in a later chapter. Certainly, the members of that conference were not all of a type but came from a wide variety of backgrounds, ages, experience and training and in a sense were united only by their acceptance of the possibility of their playing a significant role in the personal, as well as the academic, development of their pupils.

The question that concerns us here, however, is in what way those problems and all of the other parts of the 'reality' of the tutor's role in school are reflected in the prescriptions and descriptions of it which appear in advertisements for jobs, in brochures for parents, in handbooks or notes for guidance of staff and in the expressed views and attitudes of tutors themselves and their tutees. In other words, exactly how the various elements of the educational world prescribe or describe the tutor's role. Clearly, as far as advertisements for jobs are concerned, the role of the form tutor is not just badly defined – it appears not to exist. An examination of the pages of advertisements in the back of any copy of the *TES* will reveal singularly few phrased as follows (the words in bold italics have been added by us to real advertisements):

'Teacher of CDT (Allowance A)
Enthusiastic teacher to join progressive and successful CDT department
teaching to GCSE level ... *and to take responsibility for a Year 8 form.*'

'MPG Teacher of English up to GCSE level with some lower school
drama ... *and form tutor*. New entrants to the profession very welcome.'

'Head of English Department (Allowance D)
The Governors are looking to appoint an experienced and committed
teacher with energy, drive and vision to maintain the high standards of a
well-run department which enjoys very good success and which caters for
over 80 pupils taking 'A' level English from a Sixth form of 230. *The
person appointed will also be expected to make a significant contribution to the pastoral side of the school's life and to assume responsibility,
initially at least, for a form of Year 11 pupils.*'

Yet, as we shall show in Chapter 4, the person appointed to the first of these
posts – all selected at random from one week's *TES* (minus, of course, the
additions in italics) and all from widely separate parts of the country – *will*
be a form tutor, the person appointed to the second *may* if he or she is
'unlucky' (and even if not, may well be expected to co-tutor a form) and the
odds are that even the person appointed to the Head of Department post
may not escape that responsibility.

We have heard it argued that everyone recognises this and that it can
therefore safely be left out of what is, after all, a necessarily condensed
statement of the school's needs. Even if one were to accept that argument –
and we do not, since the advertisement is after all for a whole job and not
just part of one – it would not justify the equal lack of recognition of the
role in the literature commonly sent out to those who seek further details or
to candidates for interview. Nor would it explain the almost universal
experience that a candidate's views on, attitudes towards or skills in handling any aspect of the tutor's role play little or no part in the appointment
procedure. Altogether a strange attitude towards 'arguably the most important person (or role) in the school' (Marland).

Brochures for parents (now, of course, a legal requirement, with a list of
specified points that must be covered) have in the past done little better in
recognising the tutor's role, though circumstances may well be causing a
change in this. The combined effect of economic cuts, falling rolls, the
possibility of opting out, open enrolment and the present, markedly politi-
cal attitude towards education have created a situation where an increasing
number of parents are beginning to expect and actively seek some real
measure of choice in the school their child attends. This seems to us to be a
phenomenon that will continue and spread, as will the consequent closure
of schools which fail to meet parental expectations. Under such circumstances parental attitudes are likely to play an important part in the thinking
and management of schools. These are therefore going to need, more than

ever before, to show their public what they have to offer. This must surely include making some mention of relationships within the school and of the arrangements for 'caring for' or 'looking after' their pupils and therefore, by implication if not by specific reference, the role of the form tutor.

The brochures we examined, from a variety of schools over a number of years, do in fact recognise the existence of the tutor and most make some, albeit cursory, attempt to define the role. There is, however, a tendency both for that definition to be imprecise and for the position of the tutor described to be decidedly, in Marland's terminology, 'subordinate', with a Head of House or Year frequently defined as 'the first point of contact'. Marland (1974) suggests that any school can be placed somewhere on a continuum between 'tutor subordinate' and 'tutor ascendant' according to the degree of responsibility given to its tutors. This classification is used explicitly in the analysis of pastoral managers' and tutors' descriptions of their schools in Chapter 4 below.

The following – each of which is reproduced without editing, though the italics are ours – are typical of the descriptions of the tutor's role in the range of brochures we have seen:

'Pupils are arranged in House tutor groups, between eight and twelve groups in a Year, with a form tutor. Forms will belong to the same house throughout their school career. The form tutor will be able to get to know individuals in their group and will build up a relationship with them through House activities and meetings throughout their school life. Each House has a senior member of staff as Head of House assisted by a deputy-Head of House. The school is thus broken down into smaller units of 300 pupils. The availability of Heads of House will be sent to parents at the beginning of the school year, together with important dates for the whole school year. In cases of urgency, normally one of the deputy Heads or the Headmaster would be available to see parents without appointment, although some delay might be unavoidable. *Usually, however, a parent's first point of contact would be with the child's Head of House.*'

'Each year group is in the charge of a Year Tutor who is initially responsible for pastoral care and discipline.'

'The size of the school, the considerable number of classrooms, practical rooms and laboratories, different teachers for each subject and many unfamiliar faces can have an unsettling effect on a new pupil transferring from a relatively small middle school where he/she has had considerable contact with his/her class teacher. We are aware of the possible problems which can arise from this situation and thus have taken steps to ensure there are a number of people to whom the new pupil can go for advice or help. Although pupils are taught by specialist subject teachers, each pupil's first and main contact is with his/her form teacher, who meets the class twice daily in its form room for registration and usually teaches the class for one subject.'

'Each child has a form tutor with whom parents will normally deal on matters for routine contact: *for more detailed matters*, especially where parents wish to call at the School for discussion, *arrangements should be made by prior appointment to see the Head of School or Year tutor most concerned with the particular pupil*. In general, if it has not been possible to make an appointment beforehand, parents will always be seen by someone in authority, although in view of the overall teaching commitment at any given time, this may not be the teacher best acquainted with the particular pupil. The detailed organisation of the school for purposes of pastoral care is shown at the back of this publication: in addition to this organisation, the Headmaster sees every child in the School personally once a year in his room.'

'Appropriate members of staff are responsible for being acquainted with each child's family situation, health, interests, aspirations, subject strengths and weaknesses and with any problems that may influence a child's progress in school. Primarily this is the responsibility of the form tutor, but also concerned will be the pupil's Head of Year and the Head of Upper and Lower school.

All the children of a particular age belong to a year group supervised in the manner of a Headmaster by a Head of Year. The year groups are sub-divided into forms of not more than thirty, under the direction of a tutor. Knowledge of a child's social progress acquired during the course of a year is carefully recorded and discreetly passed on as the child moves from one year to the next.'

'*Form teachers* have the main responsibility for carrying out the pastoral and social philosophy of the school in their daily contact with the pupils in their form. All day to day matters, such as letters explaining absence, change of address etc should be referred to the form teacher.

Year Heads lead a Year Group, comprising six or seven forms, for five years. Heads of Year have the responsibility for the welfare, behaviour, appearance, progress and general oversight of all the pupils in their Year. *Any information regarding changing family circumstances or problems which could affect your child's progress, should be referred to the Year Head.*'

'It is considered very important at – that all children are cared for and feel valued, both as social individuals and academically. In our growing school, all pupils should feel that there are staff who understand their particular problems and needs and who are interested in them as whole persons. The pastoral system has been organised to ensure this happens.

The school is split into two halves pastorally, Years 8 and 9 under the guidance of a Year Head and Head of Lower School, Years 10 and 11 under a Year Head and Head of Upper School. These four members of staff, together with assistant Year Heads, a vice-principal and the form tutors, make up the pastoral team. In addition there is a trained counsellor who visits the school, and both he and the pastoral team are prepared to make home visits, should the need arise.'

14

'Each form has about thirty pupils of mixed ability, with a teacher as the form tutor. The senior Year tutor and the form tutors take a particular Year through from Year 7 to Year 11. There is a separate senior tutor and form tutors for the Sixth form. The senior Year tutor co-ordinates the work of all the tutors and checks on the overall progress and behaviour of the pupils in the Year. *Senior Year tutors will be glad to see parents.*'

Tutor ascendant schools (at least in terms of their own descriptions) do exist but even they, all too often, do not define the tutors' role in terms that would explain exactly what they do or how – and this in documents that often go into almost intricate detail over the structure of the academic function of the school, its origins and history, its aims and objectives, uniform, discipline and a whole list of administrative details and rules. Even the best of the definitions that we are aware of stop short at statements such as:

'The form tutor is responsible for the pupil's well-being on a day to day basis. The tutor sees the group twice every day for registration and has a longer period of time with them on two or three days a week when tutor-group activities can take place. Assemblies are also held during tutor time. A pupil will often be taught by his/her form tutor as well. Day to day matters (absence letters, requests etc) will be dealt with by the form tutor. (Please ring to make an appointment.)'

or perhaps, from among the most highly developed that we have seen:

'When your son joins us permanently, he will become part of a tutor group of about 25 in number. The teacher who leads this group will see him every day for at least 40 minutes and will also organise at least one of his lessons each week. Through the years he or she will build up records about the progress and achievements of your son in all his subjects and provide you with copies of these. The tutor will discuss and help solve any difficulties your son might experience, whether these be of the learning or social kind. Where necessary the tutor will refer a matter to the Head of Year – a very experienced colleague who works closely with the Head and deputies and leads the team of tutors looking after those boys in your son's particular age group.

Tutors and Heads of Year will always welcome any enquiries you may wish to make by letter, telephone or personal visit, although the last of these is usually more effective if it can be organised beforehand. Arrangements can, of course, be made to see the Head or deputies of the school.'

or

'The form tutor is probably the most important person for each pupil. When children join us they are placed in tutor groups and their tutor usually stays with them from Year 7 until the end of Year 11. The tutor builds a strong relationship with each child and helps that group of children to settle in well together. Tutors stress the positive achievements of their tutor group and develop high standards of work and behaviour in the children.

For day to day questions the tutor will be the teacher to ask. This teacher will also keep an eye on the welfare of your child, both in lessons and at breaktime and lunchtime.

Every morning your child will spend half an hour with her or his tutor: this time gives an opportunity for any problems to be resolved and during this time each child makes a personal file which s/he keeps throughout the time at school.

This achievements file can contain things like descriptions of work done, special events, social occasions at school and many other things. As it builds up it makes a detailed record of the positive things that happen to each individual.

As a parent you can be involved in contributing to the achievements file, and when your child nears the end of Year 7 we shall be asking you to help your daughter or son when they do an evaluation of the things they have liked or not liked in the first year.

In Years 7 to 9 tutors set aside time regularly to talk to individuals and small groups about their work and their own development. In addition the tutor meets the tutor group twice a day for registration and usually teaches that class for one subject on the timetable.

In Years 10 and 11 each tutor spends one lesson a week with the group on Personal and Social Education, as well as guiding pupils through exam courses and applications for work or study after Year 11.'

From these brochures a parent who had access to the whole range might conclude that the tutor's role (in association, of course, with a Head of Year or House) consists, rather vaguely, of:

- developing relationships
- 'house' or 'year' or 'tutor group' activities
- discipline
- teaching a subject or, increasingly frequently, a social education pro-gramme of some sort to his or her tutees
- 'matters of routine contact', eg letters explaining absence, change of address etc
- recording social progress
- being aware of each pupil's family situation, health, aspirations, subject strengths and weaknesses and any problems that might influence the pupil's progress in school
- registration

and perhaps

- discussing and helping to solve any difficulties a pupil might experience.

In a document designed for parents perhaps it would be unrealistic to expect the definition of the role to consist of more than such a list of relatively ill-defined tasks – though of course it should not be unrealistic for the introduction to that list to be welcoming and warm, and to place the tutor right at the centre of regular and encouraged contacts between home and school. When we consider, however, the documentation produced by a school for its staff – staff handbook, notes for staff guidance, etc – then it would, we feel, be reasonable to expect not just a rather more explicit list of the 'what' of the job but a fair attempt at the 'how' as well, ie the procedures by which a tutor might actually achieve a 'relationship' or an 'awareness' for example. Even an experienced newcomer to a school, who might be expected to know intuitively 'what' needed to be done, might be excused some initial confusion over the anticipated or acceptable 'how', bearing in mind the differences that occur not just between authorities but even between schools within an authority. A younger, less experienced colleague, bearing in mind the undoubted inadequacy of initial training in pastoral care, might experience considerably greater doubts and worries.

An examination of the typical documentation that we have been able to obtain leaves us with the impression that the newcomer is likely to continue to be confused. It might, of course, be argued that 'form tutoring' is a professional skill expected of any member of staff and that, in exactly the same way as the documentation is not expected to include a section on the role of 'the teacher,' it cannot be expected to contain one on the role of 'the tutor'.

There seem to us to be at least two clear counter arguments to this.

1 It is common to find in such documentation, particularly when it is written with the probationary or new teacher in mind, sections on 'the classroom environment', 'records', 'class registers', 'reports', 'discipline', 'classroom management', 'preparing lessons' and so on – all clearly aspects of a teacher's professional skills. Why, then, should it be so uncommon in comparison to find the equivalent sections on 'form interviews', 'parent evenings', 'home visits', 'pupils causing concern', 'references', 'court reports', 'enforcement of uniform regulation' etc – all equally clearly recognisable aspects of the tutor's professional skills?

2 The roles of the 'form tutor' and the 'teacher' do appear to us to be different in some respects though not, as we shall demonstrate later, in terms of the skills applied or even the tasks undertaken – one does not *have* to be a form tutor to enforce uniform regulations nor can one forget about classroom management just because one is. One of the differences, it seems to us, lies in the area of autonomy or, conversely, of boundaries. Even within a highly structured department a teacher traditionally knows that he is the person solely responsible for a pupil's progress in Maths or English or PE or whatever subject he is a specialist

in. The teacher may choose to share that responsibility and may even seek assistance in meeting it but we have an almost jealously guarded tradition of *a* teacher and *a* class and that teacher expects to retain control of any situation in which other adults become involved. In the case of the form tutor things are nowhere near so clear cut – it is not difficult to envisage, for example, a situation in which significant interaction can take place between the school and the parents of a pupil in her form without the tutor being aware of this at all, despite the fact that the matters being discussed are highly significant in the pupil's development and part of the day-to-day interaction within the form room. Equally, a tutor who initiates such an interaction by alerting an Education Social Worker (ESW) to a recurrent absence, for example, let alone by making an evening home visit, may find that she has broken an unwritten (or even in some cases written) rule of the school and trodden on a whole range of toes. Where discipline, personal development, course supervision or any number of other significant tasks are involved, a form tutor needs to know where the boundaries are, at what point information or control can or should be passed on and, equally, at what point he can be expected to receive such information or control. The whole staff need to know what is expected within the role – it seems to us that it needs to be described, and in some detail.

As implied earlier, the documentation that we have examined varies enormously. The range covers a school which can produce a lengthy document called a 'Staff Handbook' which does not even mention the form tutor, and one whose equivalent document has a section (1 of 5) entitled 'Pastoral Organisation' which at least acknowledges that the tutor has a role in discipline, extra-curricular activities, links with outside agencies and assemblies and which contains the enjoinder that 'Constructive planned use of tutorial time is considered to be a priority,' though it offers little advice on how that planning might take place or even who is able to help with it.

The more highly developed end of the range, on the other hand, includes a school whose 'Staff Handbook' runs to more than 50 closely-typed sheets covering all aspects of the school's philosophy and organisation, and contains a fairly detailed section on the 'Responsibilities of a form tutor' – at least as far as the more routine aspects of the role are concerned.

That section begins with the introductory statement that

> 'It is impossible to over-emphasise the importance of the role of the form tutor. Theirs is the day-to-day responsibility for the face-to-face contacts on which depend:
> a The ethos and standards of the school
> b The effectiveness of the school as a caring community.
> We count on the form tutor to transmit to the pupils, in the course of the seemingly trivial routines of the day, the expectations which the school has of them. For example, we expect them ...'

There then follows what is essentially a pupil code of behaviour covering punctuality, dress, movement around the building, dealings with the staff, respect for the buildings and for each other. It might, of course, be questioned in what way a tutor's responsibility for these things differs from that of a subject teacher, or conversely why a teacher's face-to-face contacts are less crucial than a tutor's. Certainly, we would wish to suggest that the setting of standards and the establishment of a caring community are not furthered by apparently distancing them from the academic context, though this objection is to a degree recognised, if not covered, by the concluding paragraph of the introduction which states that:

'These and many other expectations are transmitted, explicitly and implicitly, by the form tutor. The success of the school is the sum total of thousands of daily contacts in which teachers/tutors make demands of an academic, social or personal nature on the pupils.'

In that particular handbook, the remainder of the section 'Responsibilities of a form tutor' contains detailed instructions on various aspects of the tutor's role including registers, uniform checks, notices, care of fabric, form diaries, homework diaries, House points (merit marks), tutor periods, school fund, reports, admissions changes and so on. The style and detail of these instructions can be seen, for example, in the one on form periods, which states that:

'These are usually held twice a week while other parts of the school are in assemblies. Tutors will naturally wish to use these periods of time in their own way but the following guidelines should be observed:
1 The time should not be used for general gossiping between pupils. If there is nothing specific to be discussed with the group as a whole then activities such as silent reading or revision, for example, should take place while the tutor talks to individuals. This should, however, be a relatively rare occurrence.
2 A valuable use of the time is for tutors to talk to pupils about school events and to encourage their interest and participation. Tutors should regularly make a concerted (*sic*) effort to explain and discuss with their groups all aspects of the school and its activities.
3 Occasionally, form periods can be used for unifying activities; quizzes, discussions, creation of form record, selection of teams for inter-form games etc can all help bind the form together.
4 The form can be encouraged to use the pin-boarding in the form room attractively and might even be encouraged to assume responsibility for a pin-boarding in a corridor or landing, organising displays on school activities, festivals or hobbies.
5 A syllabus of topics to be covered in a proportion of periods during the course of each year is available from each Year Tutor and these will be discussed at the regular Tuesday evening meetings.'

One conclusion to be drawn from such statements, even in their most highly developed form as here, is that even those schools which have attempted to recognise and define the discrete and particular function that the form tutor can perform find it significantly easier to explain 'what' they want done than 'how'. In attempting to define the 'what' in great detail they often appear also to create a mismatch between statements such as 'form tutors will, of course, use the tutor period – (*which is not, of course, a tutor period but assembly time*) – as they wish' and the detailed instruction of the use of that time then given. Perhaps this merely illustrates the proposition so forcibly put to us by one senior member of staff that her school's pupils would more easily become responsible and independent if only the staff 'would do as they were told'. It is possible that one danger of writing down the 'what' in such detail can be considerable interference with the individual tutor's development of the 'how'.

A number of schools we know have taken the significant step of producing a separate handbook aimed specifically at tutors (an example of one of these is presented in full as Appendix D). Crucially, in these schools the discussion of the tutor's role tends to be within the context of a wider discussion about the nature of pastoral care, the significance of a pastoral curriculum – including cross-curricular themes – and the role of the tutor in a personal development (PSE) programme within that curriculum.

Thus one school has an extensive handbook on 'Active Pastoral Work' which suggests that pastoral care is not merely a 'rather vague commitment to the social and emotional well-being of those who use the school', but is significantly more precisely defined as being concerned with:

1 identifying and, if necessary, changing the 'hidden curriculum' within which, the handbook states, are often to be found explanations for deviant or inadequate classroom performance
2 providing worthwhile role models for pupils in the presence of concerned adults
3 directly addressing expressed pupil needs
4 supporting appropriate learning situations and identifying and modifying inadequate ones
5 encouraging pupils to make the connections and associations that would help to add meaning to their experience
6 developing specific identifiably social and personal study skills.

In this school's document it is stressed that the role of the tutor group (specifically in this case through participation in active tutorial work), and hence of the tutor, is paramount in initiating changes in behaviour and in encouraging positive and constructive personal and social development. While accepting that the tutor can be powerful in this way, this does of course beg the question of whether particular changes in behaviour are necessarily practical or desirable. We would wish to allow for, as this document does not, the possibility that not every pupil may wish to live their lives or to change in the way that their tutor might want them to, and that some may be right in resisting that pressure to do so.

One of the principal purposes of pastoral care, it seems to us, is to create and structure opportunities for pupils to make better sense of themselves, their school and their school-related activities. One way in which this can be done is through what one school calls 'learning conversations' with empathetic adults. In this school's handbook it is suggested that 'tutor talk is crucial'. In such talk the tutor mediates between the pupil's perceptions of herself, the home–school realities in which she operates and possible alternative contructions and interpretations of these realities. This mediator role is an interesting one which is mentioned by other schools and in other contexts too. Potentially it is also an explosive one on many occasions, especially if the tutor attempts, as is suggested in another school's documentation, to 'protect the well-being and needs of the individual member of the form against the demands of the institution; explaining and humanising the school's organisation, the aims, roles and demands of the staff (academic, pastoral and ancillary) and the rules and codes of behaviour of the school.' Such a mediation role could require the direct intercession of the form tutor as a protester on the part of an individual pupil – a difficult if not risky procedure in a number of schools we know and certainly with many individual members of staff.

Again, a major concern for pastoral care is the devising and the delivery of an active 'tutorial' curriculum to assist the main academic thrust of the school; a 'pastoral' curriculum which, if it is to be effective, must be based on open-ended experiential learning methods that enable pupils and teachers to examine their experiences in an active and participative way through, for example, negotiation, problem-solving, target setting, group work and self-assessment.

If learning is to be active, tutors need to be particularly imaginative in devising ways of introducing and proceding with issues in this pastoral programme. In the handbooks of schools which appear to be committed to this approach tutors are exhorted to plan both what will be done with the group and what will be done with its individual members, and it is not uncommonly suggested that they should keep a diary of work (and one might also suggest conversations, incidents and ideas) both as a record and as a tool for evaluation. Pupils, tutors are told, must not feel that 'they are being forced to indulge in a set of disconnected and incoherent activities that do not meet their daily needs'. Tutors are assigned the task of 'identifying their pupil's needs, inviting them to explore coping strategies, being ready to take on important issues with reluctant children but equally willing to postpone other matters if pupils say "no".

There appears to be general agreement, in the documents we have seen, that formal schedules of work for tutorial programmes and pre-prepared materials exist as a support for tutors, not as a strait-jacket. It is recognised that whilst some tutors will want a fully structured programme of ideas for working with their groups, others will prefer to use their own or their form's ideas. Clearly in this case, above all others, what is crucial is 'process' rather than 'content'. What is needed is a vehicle of joint activity though which meaningful relationships and trust can be developed. It is clearly not enough to offer a series of worksheets, since, as one school puts it in their handbook, 'relationships and responsible attitudes need to be experienced and practiced as well as taught (or worse, written) about.'

The schools we know that are working in this way are equally at pains to stress that an active tutorial programme, however flexible, operating during assembly time or during timetabled form periods is only one part of a pastoral and support curriculum and equally, that all teachers, form tutors or not, have a tutorial role throughout the day in school, though it is suggested that this is a role which can be enhanced by the experience and background knowledge gained through direct form tutoring.

> 'While active tutorial work is (the) formal use of time to address key needs and issues with children, very often tutors do their most important support work around the school, sometimes in the corridor, or at break time, lunch time or more importantly with home visits. Tutors are subject teachers too, and in any lesson pastoral needs are present, often in the form of the hidden curriculum, but also directly and openly manifest in attitudes, behaviour, preparation, motivation, mood, commitment, interest and enthusiasm. A skilful tutor however, will be better equipped to read the signals in normal lessons, that may act as blockages or cause disruption or poor performance from pupils.'

The supportive and developmental aspects of the form tutor's role are, of course, not the only ones defined by a 'Tutor's and Assistant Tutor's Handbook'. Details of the more administrative and disciplinary aspects are also specified. Indeed it is at this point that the enormity of the task facing a tutor becomes clear, both because of the length of the list of jobs and because of the previously referred to concentration on the 'what' rather than the very ill-defined 'how'. Even in the best of documents, for example, of a list of 26 demands on the tutor's time and skill only three – 'Taking a Register', 'Writing Tutor Reports' and 'Report/Assessment Evenings' – receive the attention that would enable a new tutor to evaluate how he or she might attempt to meet those demands. Having said that, however, the suggestions for those three might prove useful to all but the most experienced and organised tutor and are a significant improvement on those given (or more accurately, not given) in many schools. On report/assessment evenings, for example, it is suggested that tutors

- make written notes of parental comments and of any future action agreed;

- write to parents after they have taken any action on agreed strategies – and ask them for feedback too;
- find time to discuss the parental interview with the pupil;
- return to their notes later in the year to check if further monitoring or action is necessary.

One of the most detailed and explicit tutorial handbooks that we have seen is that produced by The Peers School in Oxfordshire, parts of which are reproduced in their excellent and extremely readable publication *The School Book*, which gives a vivid picture of a successful comprehensive school from the varying points of view of its pupils, staff, parents and governors.

The purpose of the Peers School Tutorial Handbook, we are told, is to provide a working reference for staff involved in the school's tutorial and guidance procedures. It is presented in loose-leaf form so that entries can be easily amended and expanded to build a record of tried and successful practice in the school. A flavour of the style and content of the handbook can be obtained from the following description of the Tutor Group which is reproduced in *The School Book*.

The Tutor Group

The tutor group is the prime social and organisational unit in the school. The attitudes, values and beliefs held by the group will help, alongside the family and peer group, to shape the student's character and behaviour in school and beyond.

The role of the tutor as a member of the group is crucial, as a figure to respect and emulate. We all carry with us vivid images of our teachers long into adulthood. The tutor group carries the name of the class tutor and this can strongly reinforce the identification of students with that person.

Positive attitudes can be encouraged and developed within the group which will influence their motivation and attainment in every area of the curriculum and underpin the pattern of relationships established in the school community.

During a significant period of their adolescence, when an identity separate from the family is being established, young people are in frequent contact with an adult who gets to know them extremely well. The tutor can serve as a reference point or bulwark to mark progress or test the strength of growing opinions and new attitudes.

(An extract from the 'Tutorial Handbook', ***The School Book****,*
The Peers School, Oxfordshire.)

The roles of tutor and of year tutor and senior tutor are described in the Handbook and guidance is given on an extremely wide range of tasks and activities including, for example, not only the administrative basics of registers, late procedures, record keeping and referral from lessons, but more complex tasks such as family contacts, patterns of community contact, student guidance, PSE programmes, Court Reports, dealing with abused children and many more.

Not just in that school but throughout the county, Oxfordshire tutors seem to be better served than many, particularly through the publications of the Authority's SPACE (Social, Personal and Careers Education) Unit, amongst the most useful of which is the *Survival Manual for Form Tutors* compiled by Marian Shaw, Advisory Teacher for PSE.

In the foreword to the manual, Tim Brighouse writes

> 'The tutor is vital to pupils in secondary schools. All youngsters see the tutor as the main person within the school who will be interested in them as individuals. Above all youngsters value those teachers who display that interest and are able genuinely and unobtrusively to assist them to develop their potential, often with a shared joke, a common interest, some encouragement and the occasional cheerful correction. Such tutors, like all good teachers, have an unquenchable optimism, an inclusive enthusiasm, as it were, which invites every youngster to enter a new world of worthwhile experience and learning.'

Since the Survival Manual is 'authority wide' rather than 'school specific' it cannot concentrate on the 'what' – which we have already noted will vary in detail from school to school – but, having assumed that certain tasks will be common to the tutor's role in the majority of schools, starts by looking at the 'how' – the ways in which a tutor can respond to those defined tasks. 'Starts by looking at' because the manual avoids the pitfall of being pointlessly prescriptive by instead posing questions to which the tutor must respond: questions about the ethos and expectations of the school, questions about the procedures already in use, questions about boundaries and limits – questions which would enable a tutor new to a school, or indeed to the profession, to ascertain how their school views the role of tutor and then to discover details about how to carry out the responsibilities.

Although the manual does not formally define the role and function of a tutor, key elements of such a definition become clear to the reader. One such element – and one which clearly occupies a central position – is that of working towards increasing the autonomy of individual pupils. Some stress is placed here on the relationship between teacher (tutor) behaviour and group response. A model is presented for work with groups or individuals, in which the teacher moves – in small careful steps with, when necessary, some jumping back a step or two if the group (or the individual) cannot handle the space it is being given to develop – from being 'energetic, authoritarian, protective, directive and controlling' to being 'unobtrusive, reflective, exposing, enabling and releasing.'

A second element is exercising good organisation which, the manual argues, will 'improve the tutor's relationship with the group, will help to reduce the sort of stress that many teachers experience – too much to do and not enough time to do anything properly – and will encourage self-discipline in the pupils in their normal daily business at all other levels throughout the school.'

A third element is fostering pupil self-respect and, as a step towards that, alleviating some of the aggravations which pupils, merely by virtue of their membership of an 'institution', will invariably experience. If tutors, for example, had to carry with them as they travelled around the school their coat, books, sandwiches, games kit and the ingredients for an HE lesson and were locked out of the building at periodic intervals irrespective of the weather, they might, like many pupils faced with just such indignities, feel a corresponding reduction in self-esteem. The individual tutor may not be able to do much about this in the short term but she or he can at least understand and empathise with the pupils' feelings and listen sympathetically to the complaints. The importance of the ability to listen – and perhaps more crucially to respond to what is heard – is stressed in this context as a quality of the successful tutor – a quality which, it is argued, will in itself create confidence and self-respect in the tutees.

A fourth element is the task of encouraging group cohesion – the sort of group cohesion which will encourage pupils to want to maintain the standards and reputation of the group, and to exert pressure on the individual who behaves in an anti-social manner not to let the group down; the sort of group cohesion, the manual argues, which comes from the tutor making expectations clear and the group understanding and identifying with them. Tutor skills and strategies listed by the manual which would appear likely to contribute towards group cohesion are the ability to empathise with the feelings of the group and its individual members and the ability to laugh with (and definitely not at) the group.

A fifth and final element which can be identified in the manual is consistency: a crucial element when the tutor is establishing boundaries of behaviour and applying sanctions. These are tasks that the caring tutor cannot avoid. The manual is quite specific that

> 'The roles of caring tutor and disciplinarian are not mutually exclusive.
> Young people have an innate sense of fairness. If they can see that justice
> is done when anti-social behaviour appears in the class they will accept the
> punishment. The mistake would be to ignore the misdemeanours because
> you are afraid it would oppose your 'caring' image to react; to ignore it
> would be counter-productive as it would be seen as unfair by the others in
> the group. Pupils respond positively to consistency . . . it strengthens the
> security of the group and through this their confidence.'

However, consistency is not, the manual maintains, to be confused with rigidity. Tutors need the quality of flexibility in dealing with situations according to varying circumstances:

'Pupils are quick to perceive the humanity and fairness of this. A wise tutor is open to changing situations and fair judgements are a good example to pupils – especially if you go through the reasoning involved and enable them to understand how the decisions came to be made.'

At their best, therefore, 'Handbooks for Staff' do make a positive attempt to describe and define the role of the tutor, and we can extract from them some common factors and essential tasks that a form tutor is widely expected to do. Three major themes appear to be present:

- work with individuals
- administration
- work with groups.

Work with individuals

The defined objective here is for each individual pupil to feel valued and of worth, and to have some opportunity to experience success, albeit in small areas. Not just in crisis situations, therefore, but through regular reviews of progress, plans and problems; through parent's evenings, home visits and attendance at school functions; through interviews with parents over matters of discipline, assessment and pupil's problems; through periodic inspection of pupils' books and files and through the negotiation of pupil profiles, our hypothetical form tutor is expected to be able to:

- communicate care and concern to both pupil and parents, gaining their confidence and support
- accept failure, both on the pupil's and on his own behalf
- control and discipline exuberant, deviant or disaffected pupils
- mediate between pupils and other teachers, protesting on the part of the pupil and if necessary defending them from the system
- instil in the pupil an ambition to use his or her talents
- encourage participation in the school's extra-curricular activities
- recognise in the pupil early signs of trouble or distress, seeking assistance from outside agencies where necessary
- support other teachers who are helping pupils in their care but who themselves need reassurance and guidance
- guide and advise pupils and parents, particularly on subject and post-sixteen options, listening effectively and displaying warmth, acceptance and respect.

Administration

The aim here is the creation of an ordered and supportive environment in which both individual learning and growth and the collective achievement of targets can take place. To this end the form tutor is expected to be able to:

- write court reports and references
- keep effective records
- draw others in, referring matters on and passing on information as appropriate
- maintain an accurate form register
- monitor punctuality and attendance (including in lesson times), contacting ESW and parents when appropriate and checking absence notes
- monitor appropriate school uniform
- collate assessments and reports, chasing subject teachers as necessary
- check and monitor individual homework diaries and form diaries
- contribute to case conferences
- accompany the form to assembly
- distribute and follow through letters, questionnaires, timetables, notices of detentions, medicals etc.

Work with groups

The defined objective here is for the pupils to make sense of their individual needs within a social framework. Understanding the dynamics of their group is therefore central to success and in this context the form tutor is expected to be able to:

- implement aspects of the school's pastoral curriculum on a daily basis
- develop loyalty and unity within the group
- provide the leadership, example, discipline and care ideally exercised by the head of a family group
- accept that the pupils know as much as he does
- gain rapport, show respect and display confidentiality
- handle questions of an unexpected nature
- yield control of the content of the curriculum to the pupils while retaining control of the process
- encourage discussion, particularly small group discussion

- relate to pupils in terms of interests and language without being seen as condescending
- express personal convictions positively when they are asked for and when they are appropriate
- encourage good peer relationships
- provide opportunities for members of the form to accept responsibility for part of the group's or school's work
- encourage and help the form if it chooses to undertake, for example, some special effort for charity or become more actively involved in the community.

The composite effect of such documents then, would be to provide tutors with the encouragement and space to move towards Marland's 'Ascendancy Model', although not the clearly defined methods and procedures that would give them the confidence to make that move. Yet even in the most highly developed of schools, which have clearly thought in some depth about the tutor role and how to define, develop and support it and which clearly wish to encourage an 'emphasis on relationships rather than discipline, on remediation rather than control', such a move may not in reality be easy. For example, in one of the documents, previously extensively quoted, the form tutor would read (the italics are our own):

> 'The school is anxious to recognise the key role of the tutor and recognises the importance of involving tutors in as much pastoral work as possible. Pastoral Heads will be encouraged to draw tutors into their confidence, when dealing with pupils and their problems, particularly where parents may become involved. Obviously tutors will play a more effective supportive role with their pupils by knowing as much as possible about them and their families. *On the other hand, pastoral Heads frequently receive information in confidence from families and children which may not be divulged.* Pastoral Heads have to decide the degree of involvement at any time from tutors, but it is their desire to seek support from colleagues as often as possible'.

That same document lists over a dozen examples of remediation strategies provided to support staff and pupils – case conferences, home visiting and group counselling – all of which are apparently initiated by pastoral Heads and none of which even mentions the form tutor.

The duality of messages implicit in passages such as the one above (which is in no way unusual or extreme) derives specifically from the particular hierarchical structures and bureaucratic processes which have been imposed upon pastoral care, with all the consequent assumptions of competence, status and 'responsibility', which arise from them. Where there is a hierarchy the freedom of action of staff at any one level is constrained by the implication that those in each successive layer up the structure know more about, or are more competent or experienced at relationships or caring, than those below, even when this is manifestly not so. The document referred to above therefore quite rightly, from this point of view, emphasises the status of the form tutor but then has to look over its shoulder in case the pastoral Heads are offended. Under these circumstances confidentiality itself becomes apparently hierarchical. But what happens if it is the tutor who receives the confidential information rather than the pastoral Head – not totally inconceivable even in a highly 'tutor subordinate' school since parents, like pupils, have a habit of choosing who they will confide in. Is the tutor then expected to divulge 'upwards' that which the pastoral Head would not divulge 'downwards'?

These questions of structure and process are important ones. We would argue that the creation of such hierarchical structures and such bureaucratic processes was a necessary development stage in the practice of pastoral care, and that through them much expertise has been developed. We shall suggest in the next chapter, however, that not only were the assumptions underlying the structures and processes often invalid but that the whole hierarchical, bureaucratic concept is now inappropriate and counter-productive as far as pastoral care in the 1990s is concerned. The task for the next few years is to make that developed pastoral expertise available to individual real tutors; real tutors with all of the competence, experience and expertise that they bring from the task of teaching, but with new and very different jobs to do in addition to those traditionally prescribed.

3
The Real Form Tutor

Natalie Peters

Natalie is an experienced and extremely well-qualified teacher. Aged 34, she has taught continuously for the past 11 years in both state and non-maintained schools, and is now applying for deputy-Headships, with every expectation of getting one. She is forceful and articulate, and as Head of Mathematics, with a D allowance, has made her presence felt not only in her own department but throughout the school.

Natalie is a form tutor in Year 9. She is extremely competent in administrative work, takes a genuine interest in the members of her own form and relates well to them, and is perfectly capable of dealing with most problems which arise and of referring on those needing further help. But her priorities lie in teaching Mathematics and in running her department efficiently and effectively, and she shows a certain impatience with pastoral procedures, form tutor meetings etc, which might interfere with departmental work. From the point of view of the Head of Year Natalie is a difficult member of the form tutor team to 'manage', since she is prepared to use her seniority to ignore or override the suggestions, preferences and requests of her pastoral Head.

John Davidson

John is aged 26, with three years teaching experience, on the Standard Professional Scale. A member of the Science department, this is his first post, apart from one term on supply shortly after qualifying. He has had serious problems of order and control in his classes, particularly with the upper forms. These were largely due to poor preparation and organisation, and with the help of his Head of Department things have improved; there have been few problems over the past year.

John is a form tutor in Year 8. He seems to get on well with the members of his form, but leans heavily on the Head of Year for advice and support in his pastoral role, which he takes seriously. He is fully aware of his inexperience, but has ideas and energy and is willing to learn.

John and Natalie are drawn from real form tutors, not at extreme opposite ends of the spectrum, but certainly different in the skills, experience and authority they bring to the job. Because of the differences in their experience and status, and in their perceptions of the position of the pastoral Head, they present very different problems of management – it is an interesting question whether pastoral Heads would, on the whole, prefer a tutor team of Johns, or a tutor team of Natalies!

A far more significant question is whether a picture of John or a picture of Natalie is called to mind when we think of 'the form tutor'. Are 'form tutors' seen as inexperienced and relatively unskilled junior members of staff like John, or as Natalies – teachers with experience, skills and status of their own? The question is an important one, since the work that might be expected of the team of tutors, and hence the management task of the pastoral Heads, will depend on their expectation and estimation of the experience, skills and status of the members of their team.

Our own impression, from the form tutors with whom we are in daily contact, is that the majority are experienced individuals with skills and status, a number of whom seem to be on salary scales significantly higher than those of their pastoral Heads. There are few probationers, since the schools that we know well prefer not to give that responsibility to very young teachers, and many of those tutors on Standard Scale seem to have had some years of experience.

This impression of form tutors as teachers of skill and experience, 'middle-managers' themselves, with status and salary scales greater than those of the pastoral Head, does not seem to have been acknowledged in the pastoral literature. Indeed there is the clear implication in much of the literature that form tutors are low-status and inexperienced members of staff, even though there are, at the same time, expectations of form tutors, for example in Marland's description of the 'Tutor Ascendant', that depend upon a high level of skill and experience.

This impression of the form tutor, formed from the pastoral literature, starts with the frequently used organisational chart, which shows two parallel hierarchies – the *pastoral* and the *academic* (Blackburn 1975, 1983; Davies 1976; Marland 1974; Preedy 1981 and Richardson 1973, for example). At the bottom of each of these charts is a group of teachers described as 'Subject teachers/tutors', 'Teacher/Tutors' or 'Members of Staff' (see Fig. 1). There are lines going to both the Pastoral Heads and the Heads of Department in the level above, to show that the two different aspects of the teacher's role are managed by two different people. These charts, taken from *The Classical Theorists of Organisation* (Davies 1976), are all very similar to each other, though they are given different labels by the various authors: 'Example of Role Structure' (Blackburn 1975, 1983), 'School

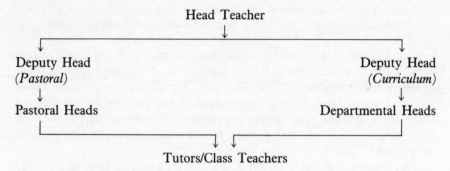

Fig. 1 'Classical' school organisational chart.

Organisation' (Davies 1976), 'Structure to show Responsibility Layers' (Marland 1974), 'Organisation Structure' (Preedy 1981), 'Management Structure' (Richardson 1973). The titles may be different but each of the charts shows a formal hierarchical structure with class teachers and tutors at the bottom. Marland did note that an individual teacher can fit into more than one level. Unfortunately his example of this was the Head of House, who is in the first layer as a subject teacher, and no reference is made to the form tutor who may be in the second layer as a Head of Faculty or major department. It is somehow as if it is recognised that pastoral Heads have to teach a subject, but not that a departmental Head may be a form tutor. Such charts are in fact gross simplifications of the real complexities of the relationships and patterns of communication between the members of pastoral teams. All, by implication, seem to deny the skills, experience and status of the tutors shown on the lowest level.

The titles of the charts make it clear that the authors using them are aware of these limitations, and intend only to describe 'structures' or 'roles'. Marland (1974) for example, stated that his chart is one of *function* only. All the charts, Marland's included, use *people* not *functions* at the various levels, ie 'tutors' not 'tutoring'. Even allowing for Marland's contention that his chart is intended only to describe 'functions', this still carries the implication that the form tutor 'function' is less significant, less important, and at a lower level than the pastoral Head 'function'.

Blackburn (1983) moved away from the limitations and authoritarian implications of vertical hierarchical charts when he discussed consultative methods of policy formation; but his circular charts are no clearer reflections of real communication patterns or the complexities of status (see Fig. 2). Even in such a 'developed' diagram, there is no way of showing, for example, that the tutor might also be in an inner ring as an academic 'middle-manager'. In fact all such efforts to show the real patterns of communication and status in schools are probably doomed to end in what Davies (1976) described as 'topological tangles'.

The impression gained from the organisational charts is reinforced in

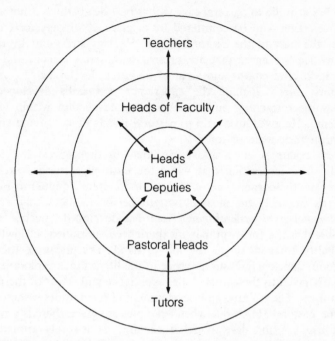

Fig. 2 'A Unified Structure for Policy Formation' (Blackburn, 1983).

other ways by the pastoral literature. Blackburn (1975), in his very clear
exposition of the tutor role, addressed himself to the 'new tutor' sizing up
his school. However, the word 'new' used here is ambiguous, since while he
refers to the teacher's experience in other schools he has (as a device to
explain the pastoral system) to assume relative ignorance and junior status
on the part of his audience.

Silcox, in her chapter in *'Problems and Practice of Pastoral Care'* (Hamblin 1981), makes some of the few references in the literature to experienced
teachers as form tutors. She is concerned with their problems and the
problems they create for pastoral management, rather than with the skills
that they offer. Her suggestions for training are not made for experienced
teachers, but specifically for the inexperienced probationer.

In a more recent paper Adams (1986), although writing on 'In-Service
Training for Tutoring' once more describes only 'grassroots pastoral care
for probationary teachers'. While he takes note of the needs of non-
probationary teachers for training in pastoral care, there is no recognition of
the skills they already have, and he makes no suggestions for training
programmes which identify and make use of these.

Even Hamblin (1984), in his extremely useful, if prescriptive, training
manual for pastoral Heads, seems to assume throughout the book that the

form tutor's attitude to pastoral care will at best be apathy – if not antagonism and rejection – to be countered by a 'planned strategy for enlightenment' on the part of the pastoral Head. He lays stress on the need for schools to use 'strengths that are present within the school', and for the 'identification of strengths and areas of potential development' – strengths which must surely include the experience and skills developed, both through subject teaching and through team leadership within academic departments. He gives little help to pastoral Heads in identifying and using these within their team of tutors.

The few examples given above are small in themselves; but we have gained the firm impression that while the pastoral rhetoric describes the form tutor as 'the cornerstone of the pastoral system' (quoted in Best et al 1983) or as 'arguably the most important person in the school' (Marland 1974), a *mythology of pastoral management* has developed, starting from the assumption that the form tutor is inexperienced, unskilled, of lowly status and probably antagonistic to the job in hand. Discussion of the role is largely about deficiencies, and nowhere in the literature is exploration made or emphasis given to the actual skills, experience and status of the majority of form tutors. The training and development of form tutors is shown as the task of the pastoral Head, but when examples are given there is a reversion to *tabula rasa*: a 'blank slate' model of teaching that is surely outmoded, and just as surely ineffectual for both trainers and trained. The difficulty faced by the pastoral Head in 'managing', let alone 'training' the form tutor – who is Head of Faculty with an E allowance and 30 years' experience, again a very real person – is neatly avoided.

At the root of the literature's misleading impression lies the fact that of the two hierarchies outlined in the charts only one has any foundation in reality – the *academic* one. The majority of staff are appointed somewhere within that, to perform their main task at the school. They are appointed to, and see themselves as occupying, a specific place in the hierarchy – Head of Faculty, Head of Department, second in Department and so on. One of the authors can remember very clearly a young teacher at a conference describing herself as 'fourth in the English department' – with no satirical overtones. This, from a Standard Scale teacher, was presumably based on length of service either in teaching or in that particular department, and reflects accurately the strongly hierarchical nature of schools and the teachers' awareness of it.

The formal academic hierarchy is reinforced by the complementary informal hierarchies of salary, experience and, to a large extent, age. With some anomalies, therefore (eg most members of senior management teams and pastoral Heads are also members of academic departments), Heads of Department find themselves leading a team of teachers less qualified, or younger and less experienced – and certainly less well paid – than themselves. The relationships are clear, or at least confused only by personalities; the authority is overt.

34

This is not true for pastoral Heads, whose team of tutors, as we have suggested earlier, is likely to contain people who are just as qualified, just as – if not more – experienced as teachers, and even paid more than themselves. The relationships between them are not hierarchical, and are not supported or reinforced by informal hierarchies. If there is in any sense a pastoral hierarchy it is a short one, consisting of pastoral Heads responsible to a deputy-Head. There the pastoral pyramid, in terms of salary and status, ends, although the largely unpaid posts of assistant or deputy Head of House or Year are sometimes created as a means of training junior staff and spreading the work of the pastoral Head.

When organisational charts show an 'academic' and a 'pastoral' hierarchy side by side, the reality of the academic hierarchy, known and accepted by all, and reinforced by salary, age and experience, infects our thinking about the relationships within the artificial construct of the pastoral hierarchy. Assumptions are then made about status and experience that have little foundation in fact. Such assumptions, as we have noted, are implicit in the early literature on the work of the tutor or of the pastoral Head, and have lingered, damagingly and unquestioned, in pastoral thinking since then.

Pastoral hierarchies were created perhaps, because schools and teachers tend to think in hierarchical terms – witness our 'fourth in the English department' for example – but perhaps also because pastoral Heads, being in the mid 1970s a fairly new creation, needed the status reinforcement of being similar to Heads of Department. Consequently an artificial hierarchical framework was imposed on a set of working relationships between members of staff who were not otherwise hierarchically linked, who had different responsibilities within the pastoral task of the school, and of whom many had major responsibilities outside it.

When we examined the salary scales and status of a large number of form tutors, our feelings about the artificiality of pastoral hierarchies were fully confirmed. In the 25 schools we surveyed there were 1256 members of staff of whom 96 (7.5%) were Heads or deputy Heads. Of the rest 66% were form tutors (see Table 1, Appendix A), which suggested that not all could be Standard Scale, and that there would be considerable differences in salary grade, status and, implicitly, experience among them. In fact we found that 61.5% of all form tutors were on the old scale 2 or above; indeed, 33% were on B allowance (ie old scale 3) or above (see Table 2, Appendix A). If we put that another way, 61.5% of form tutors had managerial responsibilities of their own in other areas of school work, and 33% had a salary grade and status at least equal to that of the average pastoral Head.

From a slightly different analysis of the figures (see Fig. 3), we can see more clearly the percentages of teachers on each salary who act as form tutors. Although the proportion of those on higher scales acting as tutors decreases, partly because of the addition of other responsibilities – for example, pastoral Heads usually have a B, C or D allowance, and most do

Fig. 3   Percentages of Teachers on each Salary Scale acting as Form Tutors.

E	D	C/B	(Old) 2	(Old) 1
12/57	63/135	175/291	219/281	294/396
21.0	46.5	60.0	78.0	74.0

(Some of the old scale 1 posts in the schools are part-time equivalents, and part-timers are very rarely given forms. This will account for some of the scale 1 teachers who were not used as form tutors. The already noted policy in some schools of not using probationers or those with little experience when this is possible, will account for more.)

not themselves act as form tutors – and partly because tutoring in many schools is undoubtedly seen as a low-status job, there are still substantial numbers of skilled, experienced and high-status staff involved. With the decrease over the last five years or so of the chances of promotion, and a steadily ageing teaching profession, even the majority of the form tutors on the Standard Scale will not be the archetypal beginners for whom the training packages are designed. For example, again drawing from real form tutors:

Peter Davis

Peter is 32, married, with two young children. A member of the Science department, without full science qualifications, he has ten years' teaching experience but is still on the Standard Scale. He is a form tutor in Year 9, has a very good relationship with his form and is respected by staff and pupils. He is also a teacher/governor of the school.

Roy Smith

Roy is a Standard Scale Craft teacher with two years' experience, having worked for 12 years in industry before training for teaching. Aged 35, married with one child, he has the background and experience of living that enables him to understand, advise and help his pupils in Year 11. His industrial experience makes him in addition a skilled, forthright and fearless Union representative.

In no sense does the fact that Peter and Roy are on the Standard Scale reflect their ability, experience or staffroom credibility, and their management may pose similar problems for the pastoral Head to those presented by Natalie Peters.

Individual schools in our sample varied considerably in the use they made of 'middle-management' and senior staff as form tutors. In school A, which is a 12–18 school of about 850, nearly 50% (48.6%) of form tutors are on a B allowance or above, while 68.6% were on the old scale 2 or above.

School B, with about 750 pupils aged 11–16, has only 16.6% of tutors on a B allowance or above, and only 50% above the old scale 2, while almost all old scale 1 teachers are used. School C, a small 12–16 school of 400 pupils, with no intermediate pastoral posts, has 50% of tutors on a B allowance or above and only half the old scale 1 teachers have a form.

School D, perhaps close to the 'average' school in our sample, with 700 pupils aged 12–16, has 34.6% of form tutors on a B allowance or above and 84.6% who would have been on old scale 2 or above. A very small number of younger staff, who would automatically have been on the old scale 1 are used as form tutors in their own right although the majority, and certainly all probationers, are attached to forms for training purposes (see Appendix A, Table 4 for details).

To what extent a school uses experienced and senior staff as form tutors will depend partly on how and why the available allowances have been distributed, and partly on the ratio of experienced to inexperienced staff. It will obviously also depend on policy decisions made by the school. Those decisions will be a reflection of the status given to the form tutor role by the senior management, either consciously or unconsciously, and will themselves help to determine the value and status of the role in the eyes of the staff – and possibly the effectiveness with which it is performed.

The use or non-use of staff with the higher salary scales as form tutors seems likely to give some indication of where the school might be placed in Marland's grouping of pastoral systems into 'Tutor Ascendant', 'Tutor Neutral' or 'Tutor Subordinate' (Marland 1974). In interviews with the senior management of schools B, C and D in Table 4, Appendix A it became clear that they have very different expectations of what form tutors should do, and very different perceptions of what they are able to do. Form tutors in school C write to and visit parents on their own initiative, for example, while this would be frowned upon or forbidden in school B, and seen as the job of the pastoral Head. In school D this can be done by the form tutor in consultation with the pastoral Head. When asked about the Marland grouping school B placed itself firmly towards the 'Tutor Subordinate' end of the continuum, school C equally firmly towards the 'Tutor Ascendant', while school D saw itself as 'Tutor Neutral'.

One further factor emerged from the analysis of our findings, which again confirmed our impressions. While schools differed in this, as in most other things, the way in which senior staff were distributed as form tutors across the age ranges in the 25 schools showed a very clear pattern (see Appendix A, Table 5). Far more weight, in terms of allowances, is given to the upper years in the schools than to the lower. This is particularly noticeable for sixth forms and accounts for the high proportion of senior staff used as form tutors in school A.

The rationale for this distribution is presumably that older pupils need more experienced staff to handle them, either in terms of discipline and control, or to enable older pupils to benefit from the advice given by experienced teachers. It could, of course, be argued that putting experienced teachers as form tutors at the lower end of the school might prevent problems of discipline from arising later, or, alternatively, that pupils in Year 9 traditionally need firm handling and positive help in choosing options. What the distribution does however, outside of such debates, is to give even further reinforcement to the hierarchical nature of schools, shown clearly by the Year Head who stated in conversation with one of the authors that 'Obviously Heads of Years 11 and 12 had more status in the school than the year Heads of the lower school'. The older the pupils, the higher the status of tutors who care for them!

From the results of our investigations it is clear that 'real form tutors' are reasonably well experienced, that the majority have management responsibilities of their own in other areas of school work, and that they are almost as likely to have a salary and status at least equal to that of the pastoral Head as to be mere 'class teachers/tutors' at the bottom of an hierarchy. To answer one of our earlier questions, pastoral Heads, particularly in the upper age ranges of the school, are likely to have far more 'Natalies' to manage than they have 'Johns'.

This is certainly not news to the majority of pastoral Heads, who are face to face with 'the real form tutor' daily in their working lives; but the model within which they work gives them little help in handling that reality.

We have already made clear our belief that pastoral hierarchies are inappropriate and artificial constructs. Unfortunately, when organisational charts show two parallel hierarchies, they *do* describe real thinking in many schools. Pastoral structures are created with the assumption that they parallel the academic hierarchies, and that form tutors stand in the same relationship to their pastoral Head as class teachers do to their Heads of Department.

Natalie Peters' position as Head of Department, Allowance D and Year 9 tutor is a clear example of the falsity of this assumption. Her Head of Year, Mary Richardson, has a B allowance and is a member of Natalie's own department; a non-graduate Maths teacher, very conscious of her lack of degree and training in the subject, but with many years of experience.

In theory, in that school as in many others, any difficulties with control or behaviour experienced by Mary in the classroom should be referred to Natalie, and action taken first within the department. Should this not be successful the matter is then referred by Natalie to Mary, as Head of Year, so that action can be taken on a wider basis. Any problems encountered by Natalie, as form tutor or as class teacher, should also be referred to Mary. In practice, of course, the nonsense of that situation is resolved by common sense, good humour and a mutual respect for each other's abilities and areas of expertise – and there are times when all of these are needed. Whatever the relationship is between Natalie and Mary in their pastoral or disciplinary work, it cannot be described in simple hierarchical terms.

One further example from the same school, school D, will illustrate a more general problem for pastoral Heads. The tutorial team for Year 11 is

Mrs Jones, Year Head B allowance. 14 years in teaching, 2 as Year Head.
Mr Adams Head of CDT, E allowance. 30 years' experience.
Mr Philips Head of Humanities, D allowance. 28 years' experience.
Mr Johnson Head of English, D allowance. 18 years' experience.
Mrs Martin Head of Commerce, B allowance. 12 years' experience.
Mr Bailey Science teacher, B allowance. 15 years' experience.
Miss Thatcher English teacher, A allowance. 12 years' experience.
Mr Smith Craft teacher, Standard Scale. 2 years' experience (described above).

This is not untypical of the range of tutors at the top end of schools. The majority of those listed here have more experience in teaching than Mrs Jones, and are on a salary scale as high as, or higher than, her own. Yet these are the people described in the charts as 'class teachers/tutors', who are 'managed' by the pastoral Head, and whose relationship with the pastoral Head is assumed to be that of class teacher to Head of Department. If this is what is expected between Mrs Jones and her tutors, then her position and theirs would seem to be untenable.

The imposition of an hierarchical framework on pastoral care may have boosted the morale and status of pastoral Heads at a time of uncertainty, but it is possible to see now, with the benefit of hindsight, that it created as many problems for them as it solved. The easy assumption of a parallel to the academic hierarchy and a similarity to Heads of Departments prevented, by and large, any close examination of what sort of relationship between pastoral Heads and form tutors was both possible and productive.

What the imposition of that framework also did and does, irrespective of the prescriptions given by a school in its working literature, is remove responsibility for pastoral work from the form tutor. It also lowers the status, not of the tutor as a person or as a teacher, since that is achieved or ascribed outside the pastoral framework, but of the role of the tutor and the process of tutoring. Tattum (1984) noticed the frequent diminution of that role in school prospectuses, as indeed we do in those we analysed in Chapter 2, and quotes one more which states, in a direct parallel to many that we have quoted:

> 'Form tutors oversee their (the pupils') general progress and welfare. Should any *significant* problems or changes occur, these will be reported to the Year tutor who will then assume responsibility.' (*Our italics*)

So tutors are seen to be capable of dealing only with the insignificant: yet it is just when 'significant' things happen that the relationship the tutor has developed with the pupil might be most useful. In a 'bureaucratized' structure, however, the 'case' is at that point passed upward.

This might well explain why Hamblin's Year 10 pupils saw form tutors as 'of low status, significance and power'. They might be seen as 'sympathetic and understanding', but they are not valued because they had 'no power to effect change.' 'Passivity', maintains Hamblin (1984), 'accompanies the lack of power and the tutor's tasks are accorded low status by both staff and pupils'.

The form tutor, Tattum suggests, has been relegated in many schools to 'an administrative functionary with a limited constructive role to play in a child's social and emotional development'. This could in part explain the frustration experienced by the form tutors interviewed by Bloomer (1985) who commented, as we note later, that their role specifications offered none of the practical guidelines they needed, and more significantly that the rules of 'the system' restricted their chance to act as effective agents. When the tutor is prevented from being effective pastoral care becomes the responsibility and province of the pastoral Head and, as the Elton Report noted in a different context:

'Taking responsibility for discipline away from classroom teachers (*or form tutors*) undermines their authority and confidence.'

(TES *17 March 1989*)

This is not universal of course. We noted earlier that some schools, school C for example, saw themselves as clearly 'tutor ascendant', saw their staff as capable of a wide range of independent tutorial action, and gave them far more responsibility than did others.

A good example of this model is the Biddick School in Washington, Tyne and Wear, the subject of an article in the *TES* (4th April 1986), where the relationship between the tutors and their forms is described as central to the work of the school. It is interesting that in this school, where the form tutor appears to be completely 'ascendant', the division between pastoral and academic work has disappeared. So have the Year or House Heads, who have been replaced by senior tutors. The name here is important since the concept of 'senior tutor' emphasises both the continuity of the two roles and the significance of the tutoring function.

The responsibility for the 'child's social and emotional development' in the Biddick School, and for translating the 'care' of the school into action, appears to have been placed firmly on the form tutors. It is our conviction that this is where that responsibility belongs, and that only by allowing and helping tutors to be, in Marland's term, 'ascendant', can care be effectively translated into action. It can only do harm to the status and practice of pastoral care to relegate skilled, experienced and caring teachers to the level of being able to deal only with the insignificant.

What we have demonstrated in this chapter is that the existing tutors – skilled and experienced as the majority are – are fully equipped to take on the role of the 'developed tutor' – or rather the developed tutor role as described in their schools' documents. What we shall examine in the next chapter is how these real form tutors see their role, what they would like it to be – and to what degree their wishes coincide with the prescriptions that their schools provide.

4
Description

At the start of Chapter 2 reference was made to an Inset Day on 'The Role of the Form Tutor' at which staff were asked to discuss their responses to a number of simulated situations which a typical tutor might face. One such situation, and one which promoted a considerable degree of heat and disagreement, touched on a number of points of principle – trust, confidentiality and honesty not the least.

'It becomes clear from the form diary that your form in Year 8, for whom you have just taken responsibility as a new member of staff – no angels but not normally in any serious trouble – are getting into more and more difficulty with one particular teacher: female, Head of RE, known to be in poor health. You start to discuss the situation with the form and it rapidly becomes clear that they are indeed playing her up dreadfully but that this is in response to what they see as her totally irrational behaviour, which leaves them bewildered as to what they are to do or to say to satisfy her. You are free when they next have RE so you place yourself in the corridor outside her classroom and from what you overhear there appears to be some substance to their comments.'

A significant part of the debate that this simulation promoted was on the question of the appropriateness of the tutor placing him or herself outside another teacher's classroom in order to overhear what is taking place. A variety of viewpoints were expressed but an analysis of the discussion showed that these could be loosely grouped, and that the viewpoint expressed depended, to a degree at least, on the speaker's position in their school. There was a clear distinction between those staff who saw themselves in this context, whatever their management role elsewhere, primarily as 'tutors': at the bottom of an hierarchy with limited status and power but with a specific responsibility for their form; and those who saw themselves as 'pastoral managers' with a wider responsibility to uphold the established procedures and ethos of the whole school.

Behind the comments the 'tutors' made there seemed to be a variety of doubts and questions:

Do I believe them, and if I do what can I do about it? Should I do anything? In fact, should I even be letting them tell me about other members of staff?

How can I find out what is really happening? I need to find out more, I need to be sure before I see anyone, but what if they are setting me and her up?

How can I find out what is happening unless I go into the classroom? But if I go in the kids will behave differently and so might she, so what would that prove?

Although it might be spying perhaps if I just stand in the corridor I can hear what is happening.

How can I help them or her? How can I do anything to change her behaviour? I'm just a tutor – I don't have any status or authority, I can't tell her what to do.

Who can I pass this on to? If I do pass it on am I getting her into trouble? Perhaps I should just lean on the class and get them to behave better.

If this is true it isn't fair on the class – they have brought this to me. How can I rabbit on about trust and honesty and relationships, if the first time they bring a real problem to me I jump on them?

The 'managers' had, it seemed, considerably less doubt. In their collected opinion:

In any school there would be an hierarchy, an administrative process which is supposed to deal with situations like this.

This is a disciplinary matter; a tutor should not be acting on his or her own, they should have referred it upwards.

There must at the very least be a Head of Department or Head of Year who should take this level of problem on.

A tutor should not in any case be discussing this type of thing with the class; it is not appropriate to mention individual members of staff in this way.

The school is bound to be doing everything that it can to help and support the teacher, or as a final resort to get her out of the school. It is necessary, however, for the school to be fair to the teacher and to work through the approved procedure no matter how long that takes. In the meantime, since the school would seem to be unable to alter rapidly the teacher's behaviour the tutor will have to do whatever is necessary to change that of the pupils, using punishments if necessary.

Such clear cut differences in the way 'form tutors' and their 'managers' think about the tutor's role, their proper actions, the limits to their action and their priorities might seem a little extreme but they are certainly reflected in, for example, Martin Bloomer's unpublished PhD thesis (Exeter University 1985). In the school in which his research was conducted Bloomer concluded that both the whole concept of pastoral care and specifically the role of the form tutor were indeed subject to just such different interpretations.

The managers (Heads, Deputies and House Heads) in the school had, Bloomer suggests, defined what *they* saw as the pupils needs and then constructed a system designed to cater for the needs that they had defined. The managers, it seems, were not concerned with negotiation or even consultation with either tutors or pupils – any form of pupil definition was, in Bloomer's words, 'not seriously entertained' – but with the prescription of procedures and hence solutions to their definition of need through, for example, documents such as 'The Responsibilities of the Form Tutor'. In a different form derived through a different process such documents can, as indicated in the previous chapter, offer a very useful framework for a shared understanding and consequent action. In this school however, Bloomer concluded that the managers 'presupposed that a mechanistic solution could be provided for what is, arguably, an "organismic problem"' and that they therefore defined care through the documents as 'something tutors *do* to pupils'.

The implications of such a concept of pastoral care on the role and status of the form tutors within a school are easy to predict. Equally predictable is that such a concept is unlikely to ensure that pastoral care takes place. Indeed, Bloomer suggests that there are instances where a mechanistic system can actually reduce the likelihood of care by too rigid an insistence on, for example, the limitations to a tutor's autonomy and on procedures for referral. Real care, he felt, often took place more by chance than as the result of carefully laid specifications for tutor intervention: pastoral care was 'just as likely to be in the playground or corridor as in the tutor group; it was likely to occur at any time of the day and not just in the half hour set aside as tutor group time; and it was just as likely to involve any other member of staff as it was the child's tutor.'

The tutors as a group, Bloomer concluded, were both frustrated and lacking in commitment to pastoral care. *Frustrated* since the manager's 'role specifications' offered none of the practical guidelines they needed and indeed the *rules* of the system restricted their chance to act as effective agents. *Lacking in commitment* since other objectives were seen as of higher priority, eg subject teaching or subject/departmental meetings, and since they did not see themselves as having the necessary skills – counselling skills for example – to work effectively as carers.

Bloomer found that there existed within the school what he describes as 'a powerful rhetoric of pastoral care' to which the staff more or less subscribed. However, he also found that this bore little relation to what actually took place in the name of pastoral care and even served on occasion to deflect attention from real pastoral concerns. The emotive power of the rhetoric he suggests lies in the root humanitarianism of its terminology. Because of their subscription to the rhetoric and because their role specifications were so vague, all of the tutors in the school could argue that what they did was adequate for the pupils and was in any case necessary to uphold the system. They could effectively do what they liked because the rhetoric allowed them to justify any reasonable action as being for the welfare of the pupils.

The pupils for the most part saw tutor time as 'boring' and 'a waste of time', regarded their tutors principally as teachers despite the fact that they might not be taught by them, and believed that they had a more personal relationship with their subject teachers than with their tutors. This is a fairly severe rejection of a system in which the school had obviously invested highly in terms of staff resources, thought and emotional energy.

The notion that tutors and their 'managers' have different perceptions of the role, place and status of the form tutor, suggested by the conference referred to at the beginning of this chapter and reinforced by Bloomer's research, supported the subjective impressions formed by our own experience of talking daily about pastoral matters with staff at all levels in schools. Through interviews conducted with senior staff and questionnaires completed by tutors in a number of schools we attempted to turn those subjective impressions into a rather more objective assessment of how tutors and their managers, in this case their pastoral deputies, 'saw the job'.

The pastoral deputies interviewed placed their schools across almost the full range of Marland's continuum from Tutor Ascendant to Tutor Subordinate – that is, from a system in which the tutor is given a wide range of responsibilities and considerable freedom of action to one in which they are essentially a 'register checker' – a view which was entirely consistent with our impressions of the schools. Most of the deputies seemed content with the degree of ascendancy or subordination they ascribed to their schools; in only one school, in fact, was there any apparent intention to move towards ascendancy as a preferred state. In any case however, all the deputies agreed that the degree of control assumed by or given to tutors in their schools varied from part to part of the work, and that the categorisation was therefore a summation, ascendancy in reality meaning being in control of most, though not necessarily all, of the work. Whatever the assigned or assumed categorisation of their schools on the continuum the deputies were fairly consistent in their responses to our other questions.

On the choice of form tutors:

Most suggested expediency, emphasising the lack of real choice when those staff who, for one reason or another, could not be form tutors had been eliminated. Where choice was possible a number of criteria were suggested (in no particular order of priority):

- past experience and success as a tutor
- counselling qualities and skills
- organisational ability
- success in other areas of the school
- concurrent views on the definition of the role

Each deputy indicated that they had some staff whom (given any choice) they would not want as tutors. Some of these were staff who were seen as having inappropriate personalities and/or skills; staff who were, for example, described as shy or retiring or having no apparent warmth or understanding of pupils. Other staff had consistently conveyed by their actions as tutors that they did not value the role; frequently late for registration or PSE, frequently dealing with other matters in form time, and often stating publicly that all tutor functions were either so time consuming that there was no point in even attempting them, or required skills in which they had never had any training.

Rather than trying to change the attitudes and commitment of those staff most of the deputies used them as tutors because they had to, but tried either to work round them – as one of the deputies said 'Good ones (form tutors) do the job; bad ones are compensated for by Year Heads' – or to work them round by exposing them to good practice within their team and trying to modify their perception and attitudes.

On the skills developed through training for, and experience of, subject teaching that could be applied, in the deputies' opinion, to form tutor work:

Essentially, the deputies argued that all of the skills and experience so developed were applicable to, and even essential to, form tutoring. There was agreement that the process changes that have been or are being introduced through GCSE, TVEI, Modular Curricula etc are particularly relevant to pastoral work and that the fact that they were now spreading from the academic region to the pastoral, rather than vice versa, as has been the attempt for some years, would in some way legitimise them. But the feeling was strong that this argument only applied to the 'new' curriculum skills and that a wide range of the personal and organisational skills needed by a tutor should already be evident in members of staff anyway, since they are and always have been 'merely' the essential skills for effective 'academic' teaching.

On the use of tutor time:

In all of the schools programmes of work existed – all 'home' written rather than 'bought off the shelf' – for use in registration time or specific PSE lessons. The descriptions of those programmes, however covered, were somewhat limited in that they described content but not (except for the programme referred to Appendix D) methodology, which it was agreed was left largely to chance. Implementation, the deputies believed, varied considerably depending presumably on the commitment and skills of the individual tutors. Little systematic monitoring of these programmes was evident, either in terms of what the tutors were actually doing during these lessons or, more crucially, in terms of the effectiveness of the materials and processes.

On the Inset and support given to form tutors:

Although more was planned for the future there was agreement that in the past training had been minimal and informal. There had been training days in some of the schools which had been given totally or partially to pastoral matters, though these were not skill based but centred on rather abstract discussion. Support in the past was described as being on an *ad hoc* basis in the staff room. Weekly or fortnightly meetings had taken place in some of the schools but in most, Year Heads were felt to have been too busy dealing with individual pupils to give much time to the support of staff. Each deputy we spoke to was aware of the inadequacy of training and support and had every intention of doing something about it. Most in their private discussions gave it fairly high priority but admitted that, at a time of enormous and rapid changes in schools, it had been pushed aside by the

National Curriculum, GCSE, community concerns, changes of management structure and so on.

The induction of new members of staff as tutors varied considerably from school to school in the sample. Experienced staff might be lucky enough to be inducted through a 'buddy' system but in general could expect to be thrown in at the deep end and expected to cope. Although in one of the schools a probationer might well be treated in the same way, in general their experience would be one of being more supported, with probationers attached to or sharing a form, or floating across a year team with some support and training as part of their general induction. However, the deputies admitted that even when the probationers shared a form in theory, in practice there was a tendency for them to be fairly rapidly abandoned with the form, while the 'real' form tutor got on with other things – a situation which the deputies unanimously condemned.

On role boundaries and delegation to tutors from Year Heads.

Actual role boundaries inevitably varied from part to part of the work and from tutor to tutor and Year Head to Year Head, since what has to be established depends on the personalities involved and their relative skills. It was generally agreed that although the boundaries were informal and rarely openly defined they were none the less assumed to be rigid, particularly by the form tutors but also, whatever the school's rhetoric might say, by the Year Heads. The very informality and lack of definition of the boundaries allows them, of course, to be manipulated by form tutors not wishing to undertake certain aspects of the role or, perhaps more fairly, to limit the commitment to what they see as just one part of an ever expanding set of responsibilities.

On the differences between tutor/pupil relationships and subject teacher/pupil relationships.

The general agreement here was that although the former might be expected to be more informal and relaxed, in reality there were few differences except in that the agendas were different. It was not even possible to push that qualification too far since it was felt that the pastoral agenda, which – from the pupil responses noted later for example – might have been expected to be negotiable and pupil directed, was in reality almost as externally imposed – by ATW type schemes and the demands of organisation and administration – as the academic one. The closest that any of the deputies came to defining the relationship they were looking for between tutor and pupil was 'a cross between a good teacher and a good parent.'

When the deputies' descriptions of their tutors and their roles are put together a number of common elements seem apparent:

- a recognition that tutors have only limited autonomy; that boundaries, limits, even job descriptions can be somewhat inflexible and more often than not determined by the greater freedom of action and clout – and time – of the members of the pastoral hierarchy
- a recognition that many tutors see tutoring at best as one of a range of conflicting demands on their time and skills
- a recognition that there has been little objective evaluation of tutors' work, but that strong tutors (judged on a gut reaction basis) are generally encouraged and granted greater autonomy and that weak ones have to be carried and, where necessary, worked round
- a recognition that tutors feel – in some ways justifiably – untrained and unsupported in the role and that they fail to recognise that it is just their skills as teachers, their experience as adults and their desire to work with young people which essentially qualify them for the task of tutoring

Although the deputies canvassed may have been content with the prevailing 'pastoral focus' of their schools, the form tutors in those same schools tended not to be, particularly where the perceived categorisation was 'subordinate'. As already noted, the tutors in three schools were asked to complete a questionnaire based largely on the table of 'indices' which Marland felt defined the characteristics of 'ascendant', 'neutral' and 'subordinate' schools. In this questionnaire (shown complete in Appendix B) the tutors were asked to pick from groupings of descriptive statements relating to:

- access to confidential information
- involvement in reception and induction of new pupils
- receipt of referrals from subject teachers
- initiating contacts with parents

- initiating action on absence
- educational and vocational guidance
- interviews with parents
- participation in case conferences
- intervention by senior staff
- assumption of primary responsibility for pupils in the form

those which most represented their present position and those which represented the way they would like things to be.

In analysing the tutors' responses to the questionnaire a number of trends rapidly became evident. It was clear that Marland's contention that a school placed towards the tutor subordinate end of the continuum, on one of the indices near the top of the list of descriptors, would be towards that end throughout, was *not* borne out. The tutor responses confirmed both our own subjective impressions and the expressed opinion of the deputies that a tutor's freedom of independent action – which, as suggested previously, is essentially what ascendency means – varies considerably from part to part of the role.

It was also clear that the tutors' responses did not vary dramatically from school to school, irrespective of the deputies' perception of ascendency or subordination. None of the tutors in any of the schools categorised their position as 'ascendant' on more than one or two indices, and many (again irrespective of the deputies' descriptions) categorised their present position as 'subordinate' on the majority of indices. Virtually all expressed a preference for the balance to shift in the direction of ascendency – that is, in the direction of their assumption of a significantly greater real responsibility for their pupils than they were presently given. It is interesting that few tutors, if any, were looking for total ascendency, ie total independence of action. This may have been because of some feelings of inadequacy but it is much more likely, and certainly more consistent with our conversations with tutors, that it was because the majority recognised the value of a second point of view, the presence of an objective onlooker and, in the final event, a higher authority to whom a problem or impasse could be referred.

Tutors' perceptions of where they are now on the continuum between ascendency and subordination, and of where they would like to be, are illustrated by the following chart. The symbol (!) is used to indicate the tutors' estimates of their present situation and (*) to indicate their preferred position.

Thus only with regard to *initiating action on attendance*, did any significant percentage of the tutors questioned feel that their position could be described as ascendant. In the areas of *reception and induction of transferring pupils*, of *receipt of referrals from subject teachers*, of *initiating contacts with parents by letter*, of *intervention by senior staff with members of the form* and most markedly of *face to face contacts with parents*, a significant number of

50

Tutor Ascendant	Tutor Neutral	Tutor Subordinate

Fig. 4 content:

Tutor Ascendant --------------- Tutor Neutral ---------------- Tutor Subordinate

*   Confidential information!

  *   Reception/Induction   !

  *   Subject referral   !

     * Parental letters !

  *   Action on attendance !

  *   Guidance   !

   *   Parental interviews   !

*   Case conferences   !

  *Senior staff intervention   !

  *Primary responsibility   !

Fig. 4

the tutors clearly felt themselves to be in a subordinate role. Equally clearly, in all of these aspects of the job their preference was to be more ascendant, and in particular with regard to *receiving confidential information*, to having a direct involvement in the *reception and induction of new pupils* (at ages other than 11+), to receiving (and dealing with) *referrals from subject teachers* and to participation in *case conferences* on their pupils that preference was a significant one (see Appendix B).

Although we had expected general agreement between the teachers in our sample on levels of ascendancy or subordination, daily conversations with the staff of the schools in which we work had led us to believe that different tutors would have widely differing perceptions of their roles. Two significant differences were anticipated: first in the importance they gave to tutoring compared with the other parts of a teachers job and secondly in the priorities they gave to individual elements of the task of tutoring.

A second two-part questionnaire administered to the same group of tutors used previously produced a surprising degree of uniformity of response in these areas too. In the first part of the questionnaire tutors were asked to assess a number of 'teacher tasks', all additional to basic classroom contact with pupils, as of high, middle or low priority. Accepting that the specific tasks do not have equal weighting, and that 'tutorship' in particular is undefined and not separated into its components, the following prioritisation does seem to be evident in their responses (shown in detail in Appendix B).

1 Keeping a forecast of work, marking work regularly and keeping records of pupil progress.
2 Keeping up to date with developments in curriculum and teaching techniques by means of reading and attending appropriate courses.
3 Attending departmental meetings in order to participate in reviewing work schemes, form departmental policies on, for example, homework assessment etc.
4 Consulting and informing parents and co-operating with appropriate outside agencies.
5 *Being a form tutor.*
6 Assisting with the smooth running of the school, eg duties, displays, care of fabric etc.
7 Taking part in out-of-school activities.
8 Attending staff and other whole school meetings/assemblies.
9 Taking a reasonable share in the school's responsibility for classes of colleagues who are unavoidably absent.

The first three sets of tasks in the prioritisation are all clearly academic, and it is difficult to fault the apparent logic of a tutor who has received little training other than as a subject specialist and who, presented with such a list, argues that the prime function of the school is to teach its pupils, and that tasks which clearly relate to that function must have the highest priority. This is not necessarily saying that 'academic' tasks are more important or more significant than pastoral ones, merely that in view of time allocation and training they are bound to appear so. For the average Standard Scale teacher/tutor simple survival, and advancement within the profession, are both more likely to be put at risk by 'failure' on the academic side than on the pastoral one, and that will inevitably generate a particular set of priorities, even though the consequences for an individual pupil may be better served by an alternative set of priorities – or at least by a better *balance* of priorities. Having said all that it is worth stressing that some 75% of the form tutors questioned gave the tutoring task a medium or high priority rating and none actually indicated, as they could have done, that they thought it was a low priority task they should not be expected to accept.

That this line of argument is valid is indicated by the tutors' responses when they were asked in a second questionnaire to identify a number of elements as significant components of either a form tutor's role or a subject teacher's role, or both. The detailed responses were as follows.

Task	Significant in form tutor's role (%)	Significant in subject teacher's role (%)
To establish a warm relationship with the members of the group, showing sensitivity to their personal needs	100	100
To encourage members of the group to accept a responsible attitude towards their membership of the school	100	94
To check uniform and encourage a smart personal appearance and pride in good standards	94	72
To record on the pupils' personal files all relevant information, keeping these files up to date and ensuring that senior colleagues are aware of any changes	91	28
To encourage good peer relationships and an atmosphere of well-being in the group	100	97
To take every possible opportunity to become acquainted with the parents of the members of the group	100	87
To monitor and guide the behaviour and work of each pupil as appropriate with regard to the comments of colleagues on members of the group	97	78
To ensure that letters to parents are delivered, timetables and other routine administrative matters are dealt with as speedily as possible and that, as appropriate, notices of detentions, medicals, special meetings, etc are passed on	97	25

Task	Significant in form tutor's role (%)	Significant in subject teacher's role (%)
To complete the termly assessments to parents, also co-ordinating other teachers' reports and giving a coherent comment on the 'total Pupil'	97	47
To support other staff – checking homework and examination timetables, developing study and revision skills, checking pupils on daily or weekly report and in any other appropriate way	94	69
To act as mediator, protecting the well-being and needs of the individual member of the group against the demands of the institution	100	72
To register the group and follow up lateness and absence, drawing the attention of senior colleagues as appropriate to pupils whose attendance record gives cause for concern	100	72

Fig. 5

These results suggest that where one of the tasks is clearly about a job to be done – an aspect of administration for example – there may be a difference in the significance it is given in the two roles. Where what is being defined is more about an attitude, about an approach, about a way of talking to and dealing with pupils for example, then the significance given will be similar whichever of the two roles – subject teacher or form tutor – is in question. An interpretation of what tutors appear to be saying then is that:

i   their role is a significant one – though not perhaps the most significant – within which they could assume a far greater degree of autonomy than they are actually given

ii   there are not 'tutor' tasks or 'teacher' tasks in a school but adult role
     tasks – or as we shall argue in later chapters, there are not two jobs to
     be done in school but one
iii there is no discrete role of 'carer' which can be set apart from that of
     'educator', just sets of common tasks related at particular points in time
     to particular functions, all of which can be approached in the same way.

Whatever the perceptions of the adults involved a crucial test of the effectiveness of a pastoral system – and within that, of the individual form tutor
role – is likely to be the perceptions of their clients, the pupils. Again we
had formed a number of opinions about the feelings of pupils both individually and as a whole as a result of our daily contacts with them. Again, in
order to test those opinions, a sample of tutor groups across the whole age
range, in the three schools whose staff had provided information, were
asked to complete a simple questionnaire.

In response to the question 'If you were in trouble in school or had a
problem, are there teachers in your school you could talk to about it?' eight
out of ten said yes.

Four out of five of those indicated that they had at least one subject
teacher in whom they could confide although one in five, therefore, did not.
For some pupils (roughly one in six) a subject teacher was the *only* person
they would confide in.

Seven out of ten pupils indicated that they would be able to confide in
their form tutor – though this meant a sizeable three out of ten said they
would not. For only one in ten was the form tutor the *only* person they
would confide in.

Four out of ten indicated that the person they had chosen was involved
with them in some form of extra-curricular activity, and for one in sixteen
of the group it was *only* through such activities that they had got to know
the member of staff they had confidence in.

As a body, therefore, the pupils questioned seemed almost as likely to
confide in someone who was not their form tutor as they were in their
tutors, and even the tutors who had the confidence of their pupils did not
do so exclusively – essentially the conclusion that Bloomer drew from his
sample.

When asked what it was about the selected confidants which helped
pupils to confide in them, a wide range of comments were made including:

'approachable'
'reliable'
'friendly'
'treats you with respect'
'prepared to listen'
'understands your problem'
'can be trusted'

'trusts you'
'believes you'
'believes in you'
'keeps secrets – doesn't gossip in the staffroom'
'talks to you, not at you'
'humorous but firm'
'takes you seriously.'

Of the two in ten of the sample who could not specify a member of staff they had confidence in, all but one felt that they had someone outside school that they could talk to about problems or trouble. What made those people different from their teachers – and these of course can be seen as the reasons why they had not come to trust their teachers – was that:

'they don't tell other people about your problems'
'they don't try to make you tell them about problems'
'they don't embarrass you'

as well as:

'they're family so they know you better/understand you better/are more comfortable to talk to/tell you their troubles'
'they're the same age and have been through the same problems'
'they are my best friend and know all my secrets.'

Building these specific comments into our general impressions, it would seem that our pupils do have a fairly strong notion of the sort of person they want as a confidant and that therefore a school should want as a tutor:

- someone who is accessible and who can create an environment which is comfortable and secure in which the pupil can feel safe about opening up
- someone who appears able to understand the pupil without making him or her feel vulnerable through being made aware of being understood
- someone who can show that they value and accept the pupil as she is without necessarily wishing to change her into something which the tutor feels is better
- someone who is spontaneous, genuine and trustworthy
- someone who can centre conversations on the pupil and her needs and is therefore, if not free from attitudes, prejudices and inhibitions, is at least aware of them in himself.

Seen from this point of view therefore, tutoring becomes a way of relating to and responding to pupils in such a way that those pupils are helped to explore their own feelings and behaviour; to reach a clearer self-understanding and a degree of self-motivation; to become more aware of the constraints in any given situation so that they can be helped to find and use the strengths to cope more effectively with life in school by making appropriate decisions or by taking appropriate action. Essentially tutoring, like the more formalised counselling, becomes a purposeful relationship in which the tutor helps the pupil to help themselves. This is not to imply that what is required is the trained specialist counsellor, but teams of ordinary teachers – with all the skills and experience as communicators which that implies – who have perhaps some insight into counselling skills and methods which add to, rather than replace, those communication skills.

The pupils' concepts of the role of the form tutor were fairly wide ranging and frequently perceptive. Indeed it is possible to argue that a significant number of tutors must, on a personal level at least, be experiencing a degree of success since, though there are clearly elements of the role that were missed out by the pupils, nothing was suggested that a typical tutor does not do. The descriptions given fall quite neatly into four different categories and include:

- in a grouping that we could call 'supporting'
     'to be interested in our work and to help us with it'
     'to try to understand us'
     'to talk to pupils about their problems'
     'to help with problems, eg to protect us from bullies'
     'to try to get the children to know them'
     'to be here to turn to when needed'
- in 'helping'
     'to teach us to get on with people'
     'to help with future plans, get us ready to leave school'
     'to help us settle in'
     'to help pupils understand the school'
- in 'disciplining'
     'to discipline us – to get angry with anyone who plays up'
     'to check we're at school and to chase up skivers'
     'to make sure pupils are early for school in the morning'
- in 'organising'
     'to give out information about school'
     'to organise things'
     'to be responsible for us'.

It is difficult to confirm these conclusions by other studies since in the literature on pastoral care in general there are relatively few studies on pupil perceptions, either of pastoral care in general terms or of the role of their tutors. This is not altogether surprising since it reflects, as Lang (1983) describes it, a situation in schools 'where more often than not those for whom things are intended are never asked for their views.'

From among those few studies on pupil perceptions which do exist the preliminary findings of Lang's surveys (1983) of the attitudes and understanding of pupils in a range of schools provide, as he notes, rather more encouragement than Bloomer's study, quoted earlier in the chapter, and concur with our conclusions, particularly in the way they show an 'increasing awareness of the caring side of pastoral roles among pupils'. Equally, however, they provide grounds for concern over

> 'the lack of understanding displayed by many pupils, the contradictions and disciplinary and administrative orientations reflected in the understanding of others, the number of pupils who would use the school for support only rarely or not at all, the problems that the attitudes and styles of some teachers present pupils with and, most significantly, the fact that it is schools themselves which seem to create the most problems for pupils.'
> *(Lang 1983)*

What is clear from Lang's results is that there was within his sample a fairly wide discrepancy between what teachers supposed pupils understood and what they actually did understand, and between the differing perceptions of individual pupils. This particularly applied to his questions about tutorial time and the role of their form tutor. Even in schools which claimed fairly well developed tutorial programmes, Lang reported that many pupils seemed quite vague as to why they had tutorial periods or attributed reasons which seemed 'unlikely to be those the school officially gave.' Equally, in those same schools the pupils' understanding and descriptions of their tutor's general roles and responsibilities were often very limited.

Even in those schools where Lang described pupils as moving towards a 'fuller and more favourable understanding' their responses seem to have been at best imprecise and at worst somewhat dismissive – certainly more so than in our own sample. For example, in response to questions about tutor roles:

> 'To stop us disobeying rules, to know what we should be doing, to stop us being silly and messing about.'

> 'To help any pupil with problems and worries. Being someone who can be trusted and relied upon.'

> 'To help an individual pupil in his or her class, to be considerate, being more as a friend than a teacher and generally getting involved with the class timetable and their teachers (understanding how they are).'

In response to questions about tutorial time:

'I fail to understand what the advantages of these periods are. Most of the lessons we had were uninteresting and uninformative. It would have been better to have been taught a new subject or learnt about the outside world.'

'We have these so form teachers can get to know you more, help out with any problems any pupil in the class might have.'

At worst Lang concluded that many pupils saw their tutors as mainly concerned with discipline and administration and their tutorial time as just another tedious aspect of the school day.

Although Shirley Ellenby (1985), in her study of pupil perceptions in two schools, concentrated on their understanding of Year/House Head roles there are similar lessons to be learned from her results about their perceptions of the pastoral care structures of the school and even of the role of their form tutors. Her technique was to ask a very open question and then to cluster the pupils' responses into a series of categories. Averaging her results for the two schools and then rank-ordering the categories, the pupils' perceptions of the role are as follows:

Category of response (Function of Year/House Head)	% of pupils who mentioned category
Deal/help with problems	80
Control/discipline	54
Advise/guide/support/encourage	41
Organise/manage	39
Support/help Head and other staff	16
Support/represent Head of House or Year	14
Fund raise/charities	13
Assemblies	12
Someone to talk to/discuss things with confidentially	11
Deal with attendance/punctuality	11
Deal with uniform	9
Deal with House points	6
Someone who knows us	6
Deal with timetable/examinations	6
Contact parents	3
Teaching	3

Fig. 6

Although only implied in managerial functions the tutor's roles of 'helping', 'disciplining', 'supporting' and 'organising', which we identified, and which can be identified in Lang's studies, are clearly also evident here.

In her detailed study, using both questionnaires and interviews with pupils in her own school, Jennie Kitteringham (1985) questioned their perceptions of form tutor roles and tutorial time, and their willingness to go to staff – both tutors and others – with a problem.

On 'Pupils' Chosen Teachers' her results essentially agree with Bloomer's. In her questionnaires, for example, in response to the question 'If I had a problem I would go to see . . .?' (Pupils were able to name up to three staff), 68% mentioned their form tutor as one of the three, though 32% did not, and significantly 66% mentioned a member of staff totally outside the pastoral hierarchy of form tutor, Year Head and senior staff. Indeed, 39 different members of staff who were not 'pastorally associated' with the pupils in the sample were mentioned, that is in fact 60% of the staff of the school.

The reasons why pupils choose certain teachers are not clear but it is worth noting that Bloomer found that the tutors he studied adopted a range of different styles depending largely, it seemed to him, on their teaching subject. 'Child-centred' tutors tended to be English, Humanities or Creative Arts teachers, while 'tutor-directed' tutors tended to be boys PE, Remedial or Physical Sciences teachers.

Although Bloomer concluded that 'style' – essentially subject background – bore little relationship to the pupils' perceptions of the effectiveness of tutorial provision, Kitteringham found that whilst most of the staff were mentioned only once or twice, two individual departments were far more frequently cited. PE received a total of 51 mentions, the two female PE staff receiving 39 of these. They were especially acknowledged by female pupils in Years 9 and 10, who explained that they:

'said they were there to help'
'could be talked to more easily as they're female'
'could be talked to on the field'.

Similarly, Social Studies staff received 26 mentions. Here it was the expertise and understanding of these two staff that provided a main support to the pupils. Explanations included:

'they know about social problems'
'they understand the problems we have and are easy to talk to'.

As Kitteringham states, pupils' motives for selecting staff to refer a problem to are obviously extremely complex. Some stated reasons for their choices were:

'because they're kind'
'I can trust them'
'they listen to you until you've finished talking'

'they talk to you like a grown up'
'they keep it confidential'
'they have given me good advice in the past'
'because she is sensible and level headed'
'they respect my views'
'I've known her a long time'.

Clearly all of these comments could be made of a form tutor, though equally clearly there is nothing in the tutoring relationship that would make such comments exclusive to tutors. Any member of staff can show warmth, trust, confidentiality, common sense, respect and kindness and the showing of these ought not to be dependent on subject specialism.

On the role of the form tutor and the use of form time Kitteringham's initial attempt to discover what the pupils saw as their form tutor's job through an unstructured 'I think the form tutor's job is to ...' question, produced a wide diversity of answers:

'check uniform and help when crying'
'take register and check for debits'
'make you feel happy'
'be like a friend to the form'
'give us things to do'
'stop us mucking about'
'be there so you can talk to them'.

To aid clarification she produced in response to this a much more highly structured questionnaire in which pupils were asked to number five functions in order of importance, that is:

The Form Tutor's job is to:
i   take the register and give out notices
ii   organise form time, activities, projects, etc
iii keep in touch with her/his pupils as individuals and their interests
iv   to discipline the class or individuals when they have done wrong
v   listen to and give support to pupils who want advice, help, etc

and then to complete the sentence: 'I think the Form Tutor should be (someone). . . . '

Recognising that the five functions chosen are not mutually exclusive, nor indeed totally inclusive, Kitteringham states that she deliberately restricted the number of options and the wording selected to enable all abilities to respond without assistance. The functions chosen for the questionnaire were, she says, readily apparent from the previous responses and were derived as follows:

Registration and notices typify the highly visible administrative aspects of the role where the interactions are generally tutor initiated, routine and public: involving the form as a collective. Typical pupil responses giving rise to this function description were 'take register', 'give out forms', 'pass on messages' and so on.

Organising the form involves a high tutor profile and is usually tutor directed, although it can be based on pupils' initiatives: in such activities the form is treated as a unit throughout. Typical responses were 'keep us occupied', 'do fund raising with the form' and 'do things during form times'.

Keeping in touch is unstructured tutor-initiated pupil activity. The tutor selects who to talk with and what about; the interaction can be a one-to-one or small group-based contact. Typical pupil responses were 'look after us in his form', 'take an interest in his pupils as individuals', 'involve herself with the form', 'make sure pupils are happy'.

Discipline is a tutor-imposed activity on the class or an individual, usually emanating from behaviour outside the form collective, but also to match pupils' expectations of 'teachers' work'. Typical pupil responses were 'keep control during form periods', 'tell off his pupils for mucking about', 'keep discipline', 'keep us good'.

Listening to and giving support to is pupil-initiated tutor activity: this was much the most frequent type of pupil response, typified by 'be there', 'help and listen', 'be able to listen and help when you need it', 'they should help you and tell you things if you ask'.

The first four functions are obviously tutor-initiated activities, the last one being where the pupil takes the initiative. The results, both of the questionnaires and of the subsequent interviews, showed a remarkable degree of consistency across all of her age groups. The most important feature of form tutor activity for the pupils was very clearly (*v*) the pupil-initiated one 'help and listen to', and this was followed by (*iii*) the unstructured tutor-initiated 'take an interest in'. The least important, on the other hand, was the antithesis of these, the tutor-directed 'organising' activity. As Kitteringham concludes, 'Notwithstanding the possible caprice of pupils who want to choose their own activities in form time', there does seem to be in these results both resounding support for unstructured pupil/teacher contacts during form time and a question about the restrictions and tensions that formalised 'active pastoral work' programmes might unwittingly impose on the more relaxed situation in the form.

In discussions of the role of the tutor within a school it is valid to ask, as Kitteringham does, whether tutors could be allowed the freedom to choose 'points of contact' with their forms and not have these imposed from without, and whether such tutor/form negotiated activities would not only allow some of the demands of the tutorial programme to be met but also enable the form to retain the apparently highly valued unstructured pupil/tutor interaction.

Although at first it might seem that there is some conflict between Kitteringham's findings, which place a high value on the pupil's opportunity to talk in confidence with their form tutor, and those of Bloomer which suggest that pupils are as likely to confide in anyone else on the staff as they are to the tutor, this need not be so. Certainly our experience coincides with Bloomer's – that pupils select their 'confidantes' in the same way as participants in any other form of voluntary relationship, eg compatability, previous experience and/or availability. Tutors on the other hand, like parents, are normally imposed not chosen, and Kitteringham's pupils may merely have been saying that 'if we have to have a relationship with this tutor, better an unstructured negotiable one based on conversation than a more formal 'classrooms' one in which we have to repond as pupils and teachers.'

What conclusions can be drawn from all of these descriptions of the tutors' role?

Clearly the tutors that we know and have talked to, and those described in the limited literature we have reviewed, feel that despite all of the prescriptive statements detailed in Chapter 3 their role is still ill-defined. Ill-defined *for* them by their senior management and *by* them for their pupils. Despite this, four themes run consistently through the descriptions – discipline, administration, support, development – four themes around which a framework for operating can be developed.

Equally clearly, tutoring does not consist of a set of skills – or even a set of tasks – separate from those involved in all other aspects of a teachers' role: the 'significant adult' role. Crucial to that role, according to both tutors and pupils, appears to be 'the relationship' – a relationship based on a shared task which is open, flexible and negotiable and is not about completing a set amount of work in a given time. It is the nature of that relationship and the actions that go into developing and using it, that the tutor in the nineties must turn his attention to.

As we have shown, the 'real tutors' exist; they have many of the skills necessary – even if only in embryonic form – and for the most part they are only too willing to use them. As the quotations from pupils have shown, there is a 'real job' to be done. What those willing tutors now need is the framework, the structure, the support, the bolstering of their confidence, that will enable them to take hold of the job and make it their own.

5
A Coherent and Continuous Task

Form Tutor's Log Book   **Form 10R**   **Tutor: John Rivers**

Monday January 19th Registration Session – a.m.
Final notice about the Year trip to London given out. Money collected from all but 2. (See list).
Letter given out about Parents Evening on February 17th.
Stern warning about litter given, after note from senior management
Photographs for bus passes – Period 3 today
Reminded the class that we are responsible for upper school assem-blies in the week beginning 9th Feb. Asked for ideas by Friday.
Checked uniform – Peter W. and Melanie S. missing some part – both have reasons/excuses? Check again tomorrow.
Lates: John B, Sandra M, Michelle S.

Tuesday January 20th
Assembly
Fund raising for form charity – ideas by Friday on which charity we should support.
Uniform check. Melanie S in full uniform this time. Peter W. still has no tie. Talked with him and have once more loaned him the spare. Write to parents if this is repeated tomorrow.
Jason D. absent again – he has had 3 or 4 odd sessions off this term already. Check with ESW and Year Head.
John D. and Darrel T. on Year detention – no homework for Maths. Explain once more about homework and Year detentions
Fixed interview with Darrel T. about Court Report. Thurs Period 3
Lates: Kevin B, Anita C. Michelle S. – warning. Talk to whole class again about lateness and procedures.

Wednesday 21st January

Uniform check on Peter W. – glanced over the others. No tie again, draft letter to parents. Told Peter Mrs Y had written me a note – as well as caught me at breaktime yesterday – about his behaviour in History. Says that he had come into her room shouting and making such a noise that she had thrown him out. Over to me!! Peter says the teacher doesn't like him and picks on him. Said he hadn't even got to his place before he was thrown out of the room, although he had said nothing and done nothing, but some others were making a noise near him. Offers a list of names of those who can vouch for his silence on this occasion. Said the teacher didn't even look round to see who was shouting, just said 'Wilson – out!' with her back to the room. Better go and see Mrs Y again. Mention to Year Head first!! Have talked to others in class who bear out Peter's story.

Had a word with David B. who has been very quiet since Christmas – sitting at the back saying nothing to anyone. Possibly some upset at home. Tried to fix a time to talk with him but he doesn't want to talk. Let it rest a bit and keep an eye on him.

Brief word with Jason D. Says he felt poorly yesterday so Mum kept him at home.

Told class that there had been a complaint about their behaviour as a group – again – from the English Dept. – again. Wanted to put that on the agenda for Friday's form period, and asked them to think what they wanted to do about the problem.

Appointment made for Stephanie G. at 3.45 tonight – wants to talk.

New pupil starting next Monday – Marie Richards. Interview 2nd period Thursday with parents and Marie. Options and timetable. Debbie P. to look after her.

Thursday 22nd January

Assembly

Jason D. absent again. ESW to visit.

Peter W in uniform today! Congratulated him.

Reminded class about agenda for form period tomorrow – ideas for charities – ideas for assemblies – ideas about the behaviour problem in English – others?

Lates: Anita C.

Friday 23rd January – Registration time plus form period.

Jason D. back again – reports that ESW visited, and that Mum is angry about the visit. Suggested Mum should come up and talk about it, or I could go to see her.

Group going on work experience – see them in assembly time – Tuesday 27th.

Form meeting – Agenda

(Debbie S. in the chair, Richard P. to take notes.)
1 Notes of the previous meeting.
2 Ideas for the charity we wished to support, and the means of raising money.
3 Ideas for assemblies for week beginning 9th February.
4 Discussion of behaviour in English lesson.
5 Decoration of form room – working party report.

The log book was begun as a training strategy in John Rivers' first year as a form tutor, when it was discussed regularly with the Year Head. He found it useful as a record and reminder, and has continued the practice. He still occasionally shows it to the Year Head.

The notes and comments in the log book are, of course, 'recollected in tranquility' after the registration period is over. With commendable restraint nothing is said of the conditions under which the work is done. There will, for example, be regular interruptions from both staff and pupils: the Year Head with the list of detentions, pupils with messages from members of staff to the form and to the form tutor. Attention given to John B. or to Peter W. means withdrawing attention from twenty odd others, and any conversation takes place against a background of demands from the rest of the class. Above all, time is the major pressure; there is rarely enough to do all that is expected in a way which fits in with the pastoral aims of the school and the rhetoric of job descriptions, eg 'to form a close and supportive relationship with each member of the class'. It is clear that time for tutorial work cannot be restricted to registration and form period time with the class.

While the notes do not give a full-colour, vivid illustration of a form tutor at work, since John Rivers takes the background conditions for granted, they do demonstrate the sort of detail he is concerned with, the people with whom, as a tutor, he works directly and some indication of his framework of aims and objectives.

We can identify from the notes a number of discrete features of his job.

1 Administration – registration, reading notices, collecting money.
2 Control and discipline – warning about litter, checking on uniform.
3 Concern for and awareness of individuals, eg noting changes in behaviour, offering time for a pupil to discuss private matters.
4 Acting as a key adult figure for the pupils – as an intermediary between Physics teacher and Peter W.; between English teacher and class.
5 Acting as an interpreter of the school to the form – helping each member of the form to clarify and make coherent and meaningful for themselves the experience of being in the school.
6 Interpreting the form to the school – the idea of 'advocacy', of speaking

for the form and its members without the implications of confrontation, eg seeing Mrs Y about Peter W.

7 Creating a group ethos and membership.

8 Fostering the personal and social development of each individual pupil.

While these can be listed separately here, in practice they overlap. In acting as intermediary between the History teacher and Peter W. or between the English teacher and the form, John will also be upholding the school's legitimate need for discipline and control. Marking a register and checking on lateness are not only administrative tasks and important aspects of control but also give information which alerts him to possible welfare problems of the individual. The last two features are not separate tasks in time, but are essentially aims and intentions which determine how the more basic tasks are carried out.

Implicit in this list of features are the four primary functions of the tutorial role identified in Chapter 4 – administrative, disciplinary, supportive and developmental.

Recent critiques of pastoral care (Best et al 1983, Bell and Best 1986, Lang 1982, Williamson 1980) have described on the one hand a pastoral 'rhetoric', which is about caring and the welfare of the individual child, and on the other hand pastoral structures and practices, which are more about administration and discipline than about care, and which serve the needs of the school and the teachers rather than those of the children. The existence of this double standard – a caring rhetoric but a controlling practice – was reinforced for us by discussions with Year and House Heads and investigations into their work. Almost every one that we talked to was concerned that the vast majority of their pastoral time was given to administration and to the control or containment of a small minority of pupils, rather than to 'care'.

This, however, implies a conflict between care and administration or care and discipline, or between the needs of 'the school' and the needs of the pupil. This is neither true in practice nor suggested by the authors of the critiques, as Best et al's careful analysis of the relationship between administration, control and care in a school makes clear (Best et al 1983, pp269–276).

There is no fundamental opposition between the needs of the school and the needs of the individual pupil, just as there is no fundamental conflict between care and the creation of order; effective administration and proper and appropriate control are two necessary factors in an adult–child relationship of care. Conflict, if it exists, will depend on how and why the disciplinary action is taken, or on how the administrative tasks are performed.

The obvious analogy of course is with the family. Administration there can be seen as, for example, buying and preparing food, or paying the bills on time so that the house is warm. 'Care and control' are seen as connected responsibilities exercised by each parent and are vested by the courts in one of the parents when a family is split. Indeed it is hard to think of care being exercised, in school or at home, if control is impossible. Control is actually experienced by the children of the family as an aspect of care, even when the boundaries are pushed – hence the classic statement from one young girl, 'If Mum didn't get angry when I came in late I'd think she didn't care.'

What we shall do here, therefore, is suggest a model for the interactions between the tutor, the form and individuals within it, which integrates administration, discipline and support. These tasks can and must be carried out, however, in ways which complement the fourth and most significant task, that of **furthering personal and social development**. This is a main task, not just of pastoral work, but of the whole schooling process, and it is worth exploring briefly what it means.

HMI noted, in *Aspects of Secondary Education*

'The personal and social development of the pupil is one way of describing the central purpose of education.'   (*HMSO 1979 Ch9 1.2 p206*)

All aspects of the school contribute to this, as they point out; curriculum, hidden curriculum, social and pastoral systems, teaching methods and teachers' expectations and attitudes. But as they also noted

'In general schools place much greater emphasis on fostering the personal development of their pupils through pastoral care than through their curriculum.'   (*HMSO 1979 Ch9 2.2 p208*)

The potential implicit in, for example, GCSE or TVEI for the 'personal and social development of the pupil' was hardly a gleam in the eyes of the planners in 1979, and twelve years later that potential has still scarcely been tapped. We can still say that in most schools most conscious and deliberate work on personal and social development is done within the pastoral system and, specifically, within the tutorial period. Form tutors therefore, through their regular contact, structured or unstructured, with all pupils, have the major responsibility for that work. This gives added point to the comments earlier, in Chapter 2, on the lack of recognition of that responsibility in job advertisements, for example.

Self-concept

Personal and social development, however, is not a 'subject' to be 'taught' in a separate slot on the timetable, nor is it solely a body of knowledge to be transmitted. Its content is 'action knowledge', to use Barnes (1976) term, knowledge owned not just by the teacher but equally, and sometimes only, by the pupils. This is knowledge about themselves, the world and their worlds, their relationships and the nature of relationships, on which they base their day-by-day actions and decisions. The educational task in 'personal and social development' is to help the pupils to explore, clarify and develop their own knowledge, including knowledge of themselves. In the words used by the Assessment of Performance Unit, personal and social development is concerned with

'... the pupil's understanding of himself, his development as a responsible person and his moral response to his social and physical environment.'

The most important part of that whole process is *'the pupil's understanding of himself'*, the development of a realistic and positive self-concept. Without that understanding 'responsibility' is not possible and 'a moral response' has no meaning. The development of a 'self-concept', an identity as a young adult, is the major task of adolescence, and support for that development lies at the heart of all social education and positive pastoral work. Hamblin (1978), in words identical to those of HMI about 'personal and social development', describes the development of the self-concept of the student as 'a central task of education', and in practice 'personal development' and the 'development of a self-concept' are almost synonymous.

The meaning of 'self-concept' is confused by the number of words we use around the idea of 'self'; self-concept, self-esteem, self-respect, self-picture, self-worth, self-image, self-acceptance. We can divide these words into two separate groups. The first group is concerned with the picture we build of ourselves, a set of beliefs we come to hold about our attributes, abilities, talents, areas of competence and physique. We can come to see ourselves as, or believe ourselves to be, for example, a failure, intelligent, dim, introverted, a bore, religious, successful, incompetent, strong and so on; good at this and bad at that and mediocre at a number of other things. These collected beliefs about ourselves are the *'self-image'* or the *'self-picture'*.

The second group of words is concerned with how we feel about those collected beliefs about ourselves; whether we like being introverted and intelligent for example, or don't care about it, whether we dislike being a bore or are indifferent to it, whether it matters to us that we are bad at Maths or good at helping old people. Our liking, or indifference, or dislike make in effect an evaluation of those beliefs about ourselves and the result of this evaluation determines our level of *self-esteem, self-respect, self-worth or self-acceptance*.

Together these two strands – the collected beliefs about ourselves (self-image) and the value we give them (self-esteem) – make up the 'self-concept' which, as Burns (1982) suggests, 'actually determine(s) not only who you are, but what you think you are, what you think you can do and what you think you can become.'

It is important for the teacher, and particularly the tutor, to realise that the development of a self-concept is not just an internal matter but is profoundly affected by significant people around us. We gain a picture of ourselves, in part at least, from our understanding of how others see and experience us, and we value that picture in accordance with how we feel other people value it. The pastoral job, the 'central task of education' is to help the pupils form realistic and positive self-images and to value them so that they value themselves.

The importance of this is emphasised by descriptions of the different behaviour of individuals with high or low self-esteem.

> 'The individuals with high self-esteem have a constant image of their own distinctness as people, are able to be realistic about their own capabilities, are active in social groups, are able to function effectively and with personal satisfaction, and have a high resistence to pressures to conform.
>
> Those individuals with low self-esteem are less capable of resisting pressures to conform, less capable of relating to others and, at the extreme, feel isolated and can neither give nor receive love and care. They see themselves as having no control over their own lives, no ability to make decisions, no personal power.'
>
> (*Schools Council Health Education Project 13–18 1980*)

The growth of what Hamblin calls a 'sense of personal power', Hopson and Scally describe as 'self-empowerment' and others (eg Williams and Williams) have called 'personal autonomy', is very much a part of the development of a self-concept. As we become conscious of ourselves as distinct and separate individuals, we become more able to make decisions for ourselves, to make choices from a range of future possibilities and to feel also that we have the right to make those decisions and choices. We become more capable of taking and maintaining some degree of control over our own lives.

It is obvious that the task of fostering the development of a positive self-concept and a 'sense of personal power' is one for the school as a whole. To give in full the quotation from HMI we referred to above:

> 'All aspects of the school and of the educational process, for example the formal curricular programme, the formal teaching and learning, the character and quality of experiences associated with learning, the attitudes and expectations of the teachers, the underlying assumptions, are factors which influence the ethos of the school and the development of individuals.'
>
> (*HMI 1979 Ch9 1.2 p206*)

The form tutor, nevertheless, is in a unique position. The form tutor alone has regular contact in a context which focuses on the person rather than the subject. While 'the character and quality of experiences associated with learning' should be the concern of all teachers, the fostering of personal and social development, and a positive self-concept, is *the* central and major task for the form tutor, but for no-one else. The possibility exists also of a contact extending over years to provide the 'continuity and sameness' which Ericson (1968) suggests is necessary for identity formation.

It is clear from the quotation above from HMI that the development of individual pupils is influenced by the 'hidden curriculum' of the pupil's experiences in the school. Within a tutorial programme, such as 'Active Tutorial Work', it is recognised that the *process* rather than the *content* is of primary significance; it is less recognised that the 'hidden curriculum' or 'process' of the form tutor's administrative and disciplinary tasks can be made equally significant and contribute to the pupil's development. The pupil's sense of personal power, self-esteem and self-concept are more likely to be fostered and developed through the way in which the other parts of the tutor's job are tackled, and through the relationship that develops between the form tutor and the form, than by teaching about relationships or adolescent development.

Responsibility

John Rivers' basic strategy for using the 'process' of his form tutor tasks is to place responsibility on to the pupils for as many aspects as possible of their school life. Decisions about assemblies, form room decoration and charities are made jointly. The Friday form meeting is chaired and minuted by members of the form. More importantly, the form is expected to accept responsibility for its own behaviour as a group, and to a degree for the behaviour of individuals within it. All of this will go some way to creating a group ethos and a feeling of belonging.

It is perfectly possible to extend the idea of pupil responsibility to cover the basic administrative tasks. Notices, such as the warnings about litter dropping, can be read out by the pupils. While the teacher has a legal responsibility for the completion of the register, a pupil can note who is present or absent. In a similar fashion the form can also take some responsibility for the welfare of its own members – as in some schools where pupils have made first enquiries in the neighbourhood about absences from the class – not 'Why were you not at school?' but 'Is anything wrong with John?' Many teachers will have had the experience of pupils sharing their anxiety about a friend, and such awareness of each other can be encouraged.

Such a strategy is far from a random off-loading of basic chores, and needs to take place within a carefully thought out developmental framework. Work on the strategy must start with the form's first introduction to the school, when the need to find out what the rules are and how the school operates creates many opportunities for responsibility to be taken. Levels of responsibility have to increase with age and as the skills of taking responsibility grow. The process is one of growth towards full adult responsibility, and the steps in that process have to be small and appropriate. Failures are inevitable but can be used to learn from – they are steps on the way, not a reason for abandoning the work; that would be like giving up high-jumping because someone knocks off the bar. The aim of the strategy is specific: that by Year 11 pupils largely accept responsibility for their own work and actions within the general framework of the school's rules and ethos. The hope and expectation is, of course, that pupils are also able to accept responsibility for their own conduct within the wider framework of *society's* rules and ethos.

A framework for relationships

At the centre of John Rivers' strategy of devolving responsibility to his form, and of his work in personal and social development, is his 'relationship' with his form. 'Relationships' has become an all too common buzz-word in the pastoral repertoire of rhetoric, losing shape and meaning in the process. There are, however, few other words which can be used to summarise the way a form tutor and members of the form feel about each other, the respect, or otherwise, which they hold for each other and the way they treat each other.

The main reasons for the usual adverse reaction to the word are a vagueness about what it means and how it can be achieved and a one-sidedness about the other words usually associated with it. 'Positive', 'warm' and 'accepting' are all commonly used to describe the sort of relationship the form tutor should create with the form, which implies that the normal teaching relationship is or should not be. Less often are the words 'powerful', responsible', 'adult', 'authoritative' or 'controlling' used. Yet those characteristics of the tutor/form relationship are equally present and equally necessary. Form tutors are adults who cannot abdicate from that position, who have power and authority over those in their care and who are responsible for exercising control. In a proper and productive tutor/form relationship the two sets of characteristics are not in conflict, but the authority and adult status provides a framework from within which the friendliness, warmth and acceptance can be offered. As in the parent, 'care and control' are complementary. For example, Herbert (1987), discussing parent and child interactions, suggests that the major factors which foster good social behaviour are:

a parental affection and nurturance
b parental control
c induction – the use of reasoning in disciplinary encounters
d modelling
e assigning responsibility.   *(Herbert 1987 quoting Staub 1975)*

His description of what Baumrind (1971) calls the 'authoritative parent' could serve as a model for tutoring.

> 'This kind of mother (for example) attempts to direct her child's activities in a rational manner determined by the issues involved in particular disciplinary situations. She encourages verbal give-and-take and shares with the child the reasoning behind her policy. She values both the child's self-expression and his so-called 'instrumental attributes' (respect for authority, work, and the like); she appreciates both independent self-will and disciplined conformity. Therefore she exerts firm control at points where she and the child diverge in viewpoint, but does not hem in the child with restrictions. She recognises her own special rights as an adult, but also the child's individual interests and special ways.'

All of that, of course, needs translating into the different framework of relationships, actions and boundaries necessary when there are twenty-five children, not just one; but the principle of encouraging freedom and responsibility within limits set by the adult remains the same.

One model for such a framework, which again is based on the family and allows the possibility of work on all of the tutor's objectives, is that described by Coopersmith (1967) as 'The Antecedents of Self-Esteem'. Coopersmith investigated the variations in upbringing and relationships within the family of children who scored differently on a questionnaire on self-esteem. He suggested that certain combinations of conditions created by some parents appear to encourage a high level of self-esteem in their children. It seems to us perfectly possible to apply these conditions to life in the form room.

The first of those conditions is 'respectful, accepting and concerned treatment by "significant others"'. There are such a number of key ideas here for the relationship between tutors and the individuals in their forms that it is worth exploring them in some detail.

Concern and care

To start with it is clear to us that concern is real, flourishing and exists in every school and almost every individual form room or classroom. The 'uncaring' teacher is a myth fostered by some of the tabloid press, and by some politicians for their own ends. It is also true to say that the genuine care and concern is not always recognised by those on the receiving end. Sometimes, of course, this is because of the pupil's own definition of what is meant by care; as one young man said to one of us recently 'I would know that my parents loved me if they bought me the motor bike'. All too often, however, care is not recognised because one or more of the other three factors in the equation given above are missing. How do we show respect to pupils, for example? By holding a door open for them; by the use of words like please or excuse me, which recognise the pupils' presence as persons; by extending to them the same courtesy we would use with a colleague; above all by listening to them, by respecting their views, values, persons and privacy. Respect is not shown or learned by grand gestures but in dozens and dozens of small ways, by tones of voice and expressions on the face.

To give one brief example, John Rivers was questioning Peter W. about the incident with the History teacher. He said 'Right Peter, will you tell me what happened?' He could have said 'Right Peter, will you tell me what **you** think happened?' or 'will you tell me **your** version of what happened?' The difference between those two questions is small in words but large in the attitude shown to Peter, in the probable response from Peter and in possible implications. With John Rivers' phrasing of the question the incident is being explored and Peter's view is seen as a valid contribution. With the alternative versions the implication is of mistrust from the beginning, and Peter's response is likely to be defensive.

All of the examples of strategies for showing respect listed above happen in schools, all are commonplace in some schools and some classrooms. Respectful treatment of individual pupils, skilled handling of difficult pupils and situations, in ways which leave the pupils feeling good about themselves and about being in the school, is not exceptional – we can both list example after example – but neither, unfortunately, is it the rule.

Acceptance

'Acceptance' is perhaps a more difficult and more complex process than respect. One of the fundamental responsibilities of anyone in pastoral work is control; in effect, getting the pupil to change behaviour which the school sees as inappropriate. For the most part this is done by expressing disapproval of the unwanted behaviour, by dispraise, reprimand and finally punishment of varying severity. Acceptance does not imply unremitting approval and does not prohibit either reprimand or punishment. In fact, as Laing (1971) put it

'If he is cheeky
he doesn't respect you
for not punishing him
for not respecting you'.

It does mean, however, that a distinction has to be drawn between the person and the behaviour and that we need to make certain that rejection of unacceptable forms of behaviour is not perceived by the pupil as a rejection of their whole self. It means that we cannot tie simplistic labels to pupils – Mary is a liar; Stephen is a thief. Mary may tell lies and Stephen may steal, and the tutor can and must disapprove of the lies and the theft. But when we move from 'Mary has told a number of lies' to 'Mary is a liar', from 'Stephen has stolen something' to 'Stephen is a thief' we move from disapproval of a specific behaviour to disapproval of a whole person, and that will be experienced by Mary or by Stephen as a rejection of themselves. This idea is very close to the Rogerian counsellor's concept of 'unconditional positive regard' – and closer still to the injunction to love the sinner but hate the sin. It is interesting that care for the person but rejection of specific behaviour is the feeling behind 'This hurts me more than it hurts you'. Maybe this is not just a cliché expressing hypocrisy but a sound working rule for applying sanctions!

Significance

The idea of 'significant others', Coopersmith's third term, is a tricky one, particularly in schools. The whole of the 'referral upwards' process in schools for dealing with disciplinary problems – from form tutor to pastoral Head to deputy Head to Head – is based on the presumed link, and the possible confusion, between greater authority in the school hierarchy and increasing significance for pupils. Unfortunately, this is a teacher concept not a pupil one, and that link may not exist in the mind of the individual pupil being dealt with. The problem is that, as Burns (1982) points out, 'the role (of being a significant person to a child) is always conferred, never assumed.' Neither the form tutor nor the Headteacher can make themselves significant; the pupil has to elect them to that position. Having said that however, teachers frequently are chosen as persons of significance, do have an influence on the developing self-concept, and do shape and change behaviour by their approval or disapproval. For the form tutor it is important to recognise that the greater the chance and ability to interact with the pupil, the greater the chance of becoming significant.

Burns' definition of 'significant others' makes that clear.

'The term "significant others" means those persons who are important or who have significance to the child by reason of his sensing their ability to reduce insecurity or to intensify it, to increase or decrease his helplessness, to promote or diminish his sense of worth.... Parents are presumed to be the most significant others in an infant's environment. *Later teachers and peer group join in.*'   *(Burns 1982, Our italics)*

Boundaries and freedom

The second condition suggested by Coopersmith is that the child must operate within a clearly defined and enforced set of boundaries, appropriate to his or her age and stage of development; the third condition is that there must be respect and latitude for individual action within those defined boundaries.

Many boundaries in the school are not, of course, determined within the form room – school dress, starting times or the number of assemblies, for example. But within the form room, in a situation involving only one form tutor and one form, it is possible to evolve a consistent set of boundaries – of limits to autonomy – which can change from year to year as the pupils grow older. Fairly obviously there is a basis, in the codes of behaviour in the room, which should not change; persons and property, the pupils' and the school's, must be respected; whatever the age of the form there will always be a need for order, for whoever is speaking to the form to be heard. What can change is the degree of supervision or control imposed, the level of responsibility expected and, as in any subject, the difficulty or complexity of the tasks set. To take one simple example, John River's form have decided to collect money for a named charity, the sort of task undertaken regularly by many forms in schools throughout the country. The degree to which they work on this by themselves, make decisions about the charity, devise strategies for earning or collecting the money and eventually get the proceeds to the charity will depend on John Rivers' estimate of their ability at this time to work independently. It will certainly be different from the independence expected of them or allowed them in the previous year, and probably from that in the next.

Responsibility and independence are not threats to the school's control but developing attributes and skills, part of the growing self-concept and self-empowerment of the adolescent, which the school, and hence the form tutor, must use positively. Channelling the energy of those attributes into supporting the work of the school, as John Rivers attempts to do, means that setting appropriate limits to independence, and allowing freedom within those limits becomes not only possible but a proper concern and normal function of the form tutor.

The question this raises, of course, is how we decide what the appropriate boundaries are for the various ages and stages of development in the school. While it would be interesting to try to devise a 'criterion referenced' set of absolutes for appropriate levels of independence in schools, beginning in the reception class with the classic 'He/she must be able to tie shoelaces', it is unlikely that there ever will be absolute answers that apply to all pupils in all schools at all times. The degree to which a form or an individual is capable of independent action, and the amount of external control they may need, will depend on levels of maturity and previous experience of responsibility given to them both at home and in school. Membership of, for example, 'Year 9' gives no guidance for this since, allowing for a year's difference in chronological age, the differing maturation rates of boys and girls and the gap between early and late maturation within each gender, individuals in 'Year 9' may differ from each other even on the simple measure of physical maturity, by as much as 7 years. The 'appropriate boundaries' for each form as a whole must be left as a matter for professional judgement, bearing in mind that it is probably better to take the risk and be prepared to pick up the pieces than to underestimate the capability of any pupil.

Anne Jones, in *Counselling Adolescents in Schools*, wrote

'In some ways secondary schools seem to prolong childhood rather than promote adulthood.'   (*Jones 1977*)

and we do not have to search very far for the reasons for this. Imposing authority and control is easier with children than with adults and if we insist on perceiving and treating all our pupils as children their wishes, demands and indeed their feelings can be more safely ignored.

One of the authors, talking some years ago to a medical audience of health visitors, nurses, GPs and paediatricians found them seriously concerned that schools, from the infant school onwards, drastically underestimated, and thereby undermined, the ability of children to take responsibility and make decisions. It is very noticeable, when working with children who are 'disruptive' in school, that included in that category are a group of children who because of family circumstances – a sick parent for example, or a single parent and younger brothers and sisters – have assumed or been given some adult responsibility and status at home. While some have welcomed the chance in school to shrug off that responsibility and become 'irresponsible', others have felt strongly what Goffman (1968) described as 'the terror of feeling radically demoted in the age-grading system'.

Boundaries and sanctions

A further question raised by Coopersmith's second and third conditions is that of how schools, and individual form tutors, can affirm and enforce boundaries without damage to the pupils, particularly to those who seem determined to push the boundaries and themselves to destruction.

Pastoral staff, and indeed all teachers, spend much of their time on matters of control, not because they are devising new and hideous punishments or ways and means of enforcing the school's will, but in efforts to apply the 'Principle of Parsimony' to the process of control – trying, in other words, to use the smallest possible sanction or intervention which will be effective, in order to maintain the relationship between the pupil and the school and limit damage to the individual pupil. This is why, for example, a pupil referred for misbehaviour will be talked with – often to the fury of the member of staff who referred the pupil – instead of being immediately given larger punishments than those that lie at the discretion of the class teacher. 'I've talked to him already – what good will more talking do?' is a common complaint. Yet 'talking to' – disapproval, remonstration, reproof and infinitely patient explanation and re-iteration – are not only the most common means of enforcing boundaries in schools, but also, in the long term and with the vast majority of pupils, the least alienating and the most effective. Herbert (1987) describes this process as 'induction – the use of reasoning in disciplinary encounters' and suggests that it is one of the major factors in fostering positive social behaviour. This does not mean that punishment should be avoided, but that when using a punishment the criterion for its use must be the balance between whether or not it might succeed in changing the unwanted behaviour, and the degree to which it might alienate or damage the individual.

Success

The fourth and final condition suggested by Coopersmith is a history of successes which can give a framework of reality to the child's view of their 'self'. The whole school, particularly in subject teaching, has responsibility for this and contributes to that history. But within the form room also, for a pupil to feel accepted and successful there has to be a majority of positive interactions so that the balance between praise and blame is tilted on the side of praise. For many pupils this will mean that the form tutor has deliberately to find ways of giving positive words and attention; smiles, greetings, requests for small tasks to be done, the creation of situations with a likely positive outcome where praise and thanks can be given. Here we can go back to John Rivers' model of working. When the form is engaged in joint endeavours, the charity and the school assemblies for example, when individuals are given tasks to do and are expected to take responsibility, then approval and praise can easily be given, and be seen to be given, and a history of successes established.

In this chapter we have concentrated on the routine tasks of the form tutor and the relationship between the form tutor and the form. Using John Rivers' 'Log Book' as an example of tutorial work in action we have identified four primary aspects of the tutorial role – administrative, disciplinary, supportive and developmental – and we have defined the main task for the tutor as furthering the personal and social development of the pupils in their form. This development, we suggested, is linked to the pupil's search for a clear identity and sense of personal worth, and with the growth of independence and ability to accept responsibility. We have also outlined one model for the relationship between the form tutor and the individuals in the form, within which the four basic aspects of the tutorial role can be integrated.

That model demands four basic conditions which we have discussed in detail –

1   Respectful, accepting and concerned treatment by 'significant others'
2   Appropriate boundaries
3   Freedom within those boundaries for individual action and decisions
4   A history of successes.

What we shall do in the next two chapters is illustrate ways in which those four conditions can be met in practice. We shall show John Rivers in action, as a tutor with his whole form and with individuals and also working at his main job of teaching Physics; trying, in those different contexts, to work within the framework of the four conditions above. We shall suggest that there is no fundamental difference between the strategies he uses as a Physics teacher and those he uses as a form tutor, or between the relationships he develops with the form as a tutor and those he creates and uses when teaching Physics. The four conditions do not just apply to pastoral work. John Rivers is one person, not two.

6
Forms and Classes

Friday 23rd January

John Rivers arrived at school at about 8.20am, his usual time, and walked in from the car park, saying hello to the few pupils hanging around the entrance and the lobby. He went upstairs to the form room, his Science lab, to drop off the armful of books he was carrying and to cast an eye over the room before his form came in.

He sat down for a moment with his timetable for the day, and the notes he had made the evening before.

Period   1   Tutor period
         2   Course supervision – Martin W, Alan O, Harjit P.
      3/4   GCSE Physics – Year 10 group
         5   Preparation time (See Marie – 1.15 Lab)
         6   Maths – Year 8 group
      7/8   Process Science – Year 7 group

There was nothing unusual in the day apart from the appointment he had made in Period 5 to see one of the girls from his form. He had been wondering about Marie for some time, since she had been much quieter than usual, almost surly, and with a tendency to snap at others in the form. One or two of his colleagues had commented on the difference in her but he had said nothing to Marie since he had felt that until she wanted to talk she would resent him asking questions. What he had done was to give her the opportunity once or twice to speak briefly to him on her own – and the last time he had done this she had used the chance and asked to talk to him. Well, at least now she wanted to talk. He moved through to the store room to sort out the boxes for the Year 10 group in Period 3, and to check the master gas and water taps and the switch to the electricity supply. It was a nuisance having to use a lab as a classroom – it was all too easy for some idiot to play around, particularly if any equipment had been left or put out.

By the time he got down to the staffroom most of his colleagues were there, waiting for the morning 'briefing session' by the Head.

As he sat down Ray Davies, a CDT teacher, came over to him to talk about the behaviour of Darrel T in the workshop on the previous day. Ray described Darrel as 'a danger to others in the workshop'. He had gone around tormenting other pupils who were using pieces of equipment, and had tried to involve them in 'fencing' games with a piece of wood in his hand. He had been put into detention for this, but he had been told repeatedly about the stupidity of his behaviour over the last few weeks and unless something changed he would be excluded from the workshops on the grounds of safety. John promised to 'have a word' with Darrel and to add his weight to the warning. The briefing over, he made his way back to the lab as the bell rang for beginning of school.

Friday 23rd January is a normal day for John Rivers in the sense that none of the work on that day is outside his normal range. Built into it, and pushed into the spaces between the periods, is a representative cross-section of his day-to-day work, both as a science teacher and as a form tutor. He has six distinct jobs to do:

- to conduct a registration period with administrative and organisational aspects
- to conduct a form period – on this occasion a form meeting
- to conduct a profiling session for three pupils in his form
- to interview a pupil – in his one 'free' period – who had asked for his help and who therefore presumably had some difficulties
- to find time to see Darrel T to follow up the conversation with Ray Davies
- to teach his two subjects in five periods out of the eight.

At first glance the jobs for Friday 23rd seem widely different. They appear to demand a wide range of teaching and tutorial skills – mastery of subject; class organisation; profiling; counselling; disciplinary. Nevertheless there are firm connecting links between them, in aims and in methodology, and while they may be different they are not disparate; there is no contradiction of principle between them.

What we must do to demonstrate this is to focus on the process of each activity, not on the content; on the *how* rather than the *what*. We need to examine:

- how each activity is handled in practice
- the extent to which it differs from the others in aims and intentions
- what skills are needed for each activity
- whether the skills used in one are also relevant to another.

Period 1

John's first session, combined with a registration time to give about an hour, was the tutor period. As the form came into the room John did his usual head count. Twenty-three pupils were present, which meant that one was absent or late. John D was responsible that week for giving him the names of anyone not there at the start of registration, so he could wait until then to find out who it was. He noticed that Jason was back today and called him over. Jason produced a note from his mother explaining that he had not felt well the previous day, but said Mum was 'livid' about the ESW calling. John agreed with him that it wasn't always a good thing to have happen, and suggested that Jason ask his mother to come up to school to talk about his absences – or perhaps she would rather Mr Rivers visited her? Jason promised to carry the message.

The agenda for the meeting had been typed and copied:

Form meeting – Friday 23rd January
Chair: Sandra M.   Scribe: Richard P.
Agenda

1 Notes of the previous meeting.
2 Decoration of form room – working party report.
3 Ideas for the charity we wished to support, and the means of raising money.
4 Ideas for assemblies for week beginning 9th February.
5 Discussion of behaviour in English lesson.

John gave out the slips of paper himself, walking round the form room exchanging a word with one or two pupils, particularly those going on work experience. When he came to Darrel T he told him to come to the form room at break time, explaining that he wanted to talk to him briefly about the situation in CDT. John D reported that Sandra M was not there, but as he spoke she came into the room. John lifted his eyebrows at her and she came over to apologise for being late and to give him the reason.

While the form looked through the agenda, John completed his register. Sandra M came out to take her place as Chair of the Form meeting, Richard P came out with some paper for notes and John moved to the back of the room.

Let us move for a moment to the position of an observer on the wall of the form room. Sandra M is 'in the chair' in more than one sense, sitting in John's place behind and in the centre of the raised demonstration bench. Richard P is also behind the demonstration desk at one end, reading the minutes of the last form meeting, which took place before Christmas. The pupils are sitting on stools behind each of the work benches, facing the demonstration bench. Those who would normally have their backs to the demonstration bench have moved round to the end of the work benches. John is at the back of the room, behind them, visible to the Chair and secretary but not to the rest of the form, although they are aware of his presence. The focus of attention is on Sandra and Richard, Chair and

Secretary. There is an acceptance of the formal procedures, and of Sandra's authority, since the pupils have some years of practice; the Chair, and the responsibility of taking notes of decisions made or intended actions, are shared among all members of the form. John Rivers retains a right of veto of any decision made, but uses this as little as possible.

The first three items were worked through rapidly but at Item 4, 'Ideas for assemblies', the process stumbled. There were few ideas produced, in spite of exhortation from Sandra, and John had to intervene. Through the 'Chair' he suggested that they spent a couple of minutes thinking and making notes of their own ideas, that they then got into their usual groups and spent five minutes talking this through and sharing any ideas, and that they came together after that to share any ideas produced. This is a standard strategy that John frequently uses and here it allowed the pupils to try out one or two ideas within the small group, come to some agreement, and support each other in pressing for their ideas to be adopted. It also enabled one of the groups to volunteer to be responsible for the assemblies, calling on others in the form where necessary. Sandra as 'Chair' pointed out that the same group had volunteered last time, and reference was made to notes of form meetings last term. It was eventually agreed that the volunteer group would be responsible for the organisation of the assemblies, but that others who had taken little part in them last time should be the main performers.

To work through this process takes time; a far more efficient system for deciding who and what would be done would be for John to keep a list of those who had taken part and for the assemblies to be taken in turn. However, this would make John responsible, and take that responsibility away from the form as a whole. It is obviously important that the assemblies are prepared, but far more important are the lessons learned from the process of making that happen; lessons about discussion, about sharing ideas, about accepting 'adhocratic' leadership, of being responsible for their own actions within a framework.

At Item 5, 'Behaviour in the English lesson', Sandra M asked John to introduce the subject. John came out to the front of the classroom and reminded the form that they had talked about this a few weeks ago when the last instance of poor behaviour in the English lesson had been reported. The suggested action then, he said, had been for the form to apologise to the teacher and to try not to repeat the behaviour. The apology had been given at a special session after school, but this had obviously not been sufficient. He repeated the recent conversation he had had with the English teacher, Mr Smithers, suggesting that like the last time this was not one or two individuals being disruptive, but that the whole form had apparently been awkward and unco-operative. He stressed that such behaviour was not acceptable. He had put this item on the agenda, he said, because some positive action had to be taken, and he wanted each pupil to have a chance to think how the disruption started and to examine their own contribution. He also wanted some ideas about dealing with the lesson differently next week. To begin with however, he asked Sandra if she would establish whether the form agreed that the lesson had been disrupted and how they felt about their own behaviour.

Sandra took over the meeting once more and put that question to the form. Since there was no initial response she used the method applied to the previous item and asked them to discuss this briefly with their neighbour or with the one or two people sitting near them. This produced a buzz of conversation as the pupils took themselves back to that particular lesson and remembered their own actions, feelings and reactions. After three or four minutes Sandra asked for comment on the question and this time one or two were able to reply, having rehearsed their response in the smaller group. A general discussion took place.

John is still sitting silently at the back of the room. His presence there reinforces Sandra's authority and makes sure that the form remains orderly and focused on the task. In one sense, since the methodology is established practice, Sandra is merely acting as John's agent, but she and the others gained experience in and practiced forms of public discussion. Inevitably too, the content of the discussion, what was actually said, is influenced by John's presence, as is the form of language used. The freedom to state an honest opinion in the form meeting, or to argue a point of view, is not extended to licence to say anything in any sort of language. John does not have to spell this out repeatedly because the members of the form have been experiencing this discipline from their first year in the school, and the lesson, very largely, has been learned. The area of freedom has grown as the form has matured but the boundaries are still there, reinforced by the school's authority.

John's question produced varied responses, and Sandra asked John to comment on these. He described the replies as falling into four main groups.
a There was a degree of disruption in that particular lesson.
b The disruption was not too severe and certainly not as serious as had been described.
c It was not the whole form but a particular group of pupils, at least at first.
d The disruption had only become general and more serious when the whole group were threatened with punishment because of the behaviour of a few.

These he summarised as – 'We weren't that bad' (ie it didn't happen really); 'It wasn't me it was him – or her' (it did happen but it was someone else); 'In any case he (the teacher) asked for it, it was all his fault' (it didn't happen, it was someone else and we were right to do it). Since John had pointed out the contradictions in these standard defensive positions many times before his summary raised some smiles.

He went on to say, as he had said to them before, that when a piece of disruption started, by one or two members of the form perhaps, how they themselves reacted to that behaviour was significant in deciding whether the behaviour continued or fizzled out. To do nothing but sit back and watch the show, or to smile at the actions could be seen as colluding with and encouraging whatever was going on, so that one person being rude or unco-operative might feel that they were doing so with the support of those around them. With Sandra's permission he suggested that bearing this in mind the members of the form might think for a moment about their own actions on that occasion, how they felt about what had happened, and then talk in their working groups about what each had done and felt. 'We might then share some ideas from those conversations,' he said.

The process of exploration with the form arrives here at a critical point. John's objective in working through that process is not to investigate what happened, nor to decide on who was guilty and issue punishment – he is playing neither a detective nor a judge – but to try to change the behaviour of the form. For that it is more important that they acknowledge their own responsibility to themselves and each other than for John to find out who did what. For this reason he does not challenge any of the statements, since he wants to move on to possible actions. If he had been judgemental the most likely result would have been a defensive reaction on the part of some members of the form which would stop them from examining their own contribution to the disruption with any sincerity. Others would also stop examining their own behaviour from the feeling that 'the enquiry' didn't concern them. He must, as we noted in the previous chapter, suspend both belief and disbelief, and listen without trying to assess degrees of responsibility between the members of the form.

There is a further judgemental trap to avoid here. The discussion brings out a significant point about John's relationships with his colleagues and with the form, and the difficult, sometimes conflicting, areas of staff loyalty and honesty with the pupils, which we shall discuss more fully in a later chapter. It seems certain that the pupils, or some of them, did not behave well. But there was also a strong likelihood that Mr Smithers mishandled a situation and bore some responsibility for the level of disruption. The pupils hinted at this and John's knowledge of that teacher confirmed the possibility. His loyalty to his colleague, in the ethos of his school and staffroom, stops him from agreeing openly that the teacher was in any way to blame. But he also has a duty not to be dishonest with the form and not to create in them as a group a sense of injustice, a feeling that they were being blamed and perhaps punished for more than they did, since this would also prevent them from examining honestly their own actions.

John had taken over control of the process at this point and he allowed the form five minutes or so before stopping the conversations. He repeated that he did not want to hear what each person had done but asked them to agree that it was probable that the great majority had, in some way, been involved – had at least smiled at the actions of others, had felt angry at what Mr Smithers had said, had shown their reactions in some way – so that Mr Smithers was left with the feeling that the whole form had been antagonistic. This produced at least some murmurs of agreement, nodding of heads and general acceptance. The next step, John said, was to look at what might happen in the next English lesson and at how they might 'manage' the situation so that the trouble was not repeated. Perhaps, he said to Sandra M., they could discuss that in their pairs or threes and share their conclusions. John then returned to his seat at the back of the room.

There is a coherent framework to the process John has been working through with his form. In the first place he remains firmly in charge; in no sense does he abdicate from his position as the adult responsible for them with an accepted and legitimate authority over them. He assumes, by his interventions and by the precedent of established practices, responsibility for the structure of what goes on, for guiding the process and to some degree for the content. The outcomes and decisions are left to the form but since this is a matter of school discipline even those are expected to fit within a usual pattern. John sets the boundaries therefore, by maintaining his adult role and by establishing norms of behaviour, but the form are given freedom of action within those boundaries.

Secondly, John listens to and accepts the statements that are made. Whether he agrees with them or not, whether he finds them simplistic, confused, self-contradictory and easy to take apart – and many of them will be all of these – is irrelevant; unless he respects as serious comment the opinions and views given, genuine communication and exploration will cease. Confrontation and challenge, investigation and reproof, at least while the situation is being explored, are inappropriate and non-productive.

Thirdly, he is consistent throughout in placing the responsibility for resolving the situation firmly onto the form group. The message he puts over is – 'You have a problem for which you seem to be, in part at least, responsible for creating. What are you going to do about it; how are you going to resolve it?' This is why he raised the matter as an item on the agenda of the form meeting, a forum where the chair is taken by a member of the form and where discussion and the statement of opinion is expected. The fact that Sandra M. remains in the chair throughout, and that John defers to her, reinforces the form's responsibility for the outcome. John's interventions can be seen as those of 'expert witness', trying to develop the form's understanding of what they are saying and the implications of their attitudes. He is 'called in' by the Chair to assist, and his authority – in the sense of 'one who knows' as well as of 'one who is in charge' – is recognised by the pupils, as they recognise also his wish to help them.

The final task will be to help the form to evaluate the various suggestions for action that are produced by the debate. This too will be done without prescription or dictation although, again in the position of 'expert witness', he will have to advise the form on probable effectiveness, and on whether the suggested action falls within school expectations.

John's framework, therefore, is one where listening, without critical comment, is followed by questions and strategies to develop further understanding and clarification, and finally by evaluated action. It is based on, and is dependent upon, his 'significance' to the form and a relationship of trust deliberately built up over a number of years. Within the framework at least three of the four conditions listed at the end of Chapter 5 are met; there is respectful and accepting treatment of the form, boundaries are established and there is freedom, of action and decision, within them.

A basic strategy used in the process is that of a movement from individual thought, and perhaps jotting down of ideas, to a discussion in small groups and then to a sharing or pooling of ideas with the form as a whole. Since it is a strategy that John frequently uses it is worth looking at it in more detail and at the teaching skills needed to put it into operation.

John begins with pupils having a few minutes to think up ideas on their own and make any notes they wish. These few minutes on their own are important, since they allow the pupils a period of reflection which enables them to 'start from where *they* are' with their own thoughts and ideas, and gives them the chance to go into the group with something to contribute. John's part in this is to make clear what it is they have to think about and to ensure that there is a period of silence so that they have a chance to think without interruption.

After a minute or so the pupils move into their regular, small working groups. These present groups, of five or six pupils, were established at the beginning of the school year; in the previous year they had worked in slightly different groups. The group compositions are based to some extent on pupil preferences but are ultimately determined by John; this allows him to break up or avoid intractably unprofitable combinations of pupils and also enables him to place appropriately those rather isolated pupils who are unlikely to be chosen by any others. The group stays together for at least a term, often rather longer, so that the skills of working together can develop and difficulties can be overcome, rather than avoided by movement to another group.

Movement into the groups is something in which the form have considerable practice since the groups are used frequently in the tutor periods and it is now, after John's insistence over years, done without fuss. The pupils know also that they need to be able to see each other to talk properly, so they form round the ends of benches or in circles in the spaces and avoid, for example, sitting in straight lines.

We have emphasised the idea of practice and the frequent use of the groups because working in a small group – discussing and sharing ideas, sticking to an agenda and a task and producing some results – is a process which demands skills and experience. This particular form have developed many of those skills and can handle sophisticated ideas and materials in this way, but for the most part John still keeps the task for the group fairly simple and the time in which the group works together fairly short. This not only allows him to keep control but ensures that the work of the group is focused and to the point, and is particularly necessary with younger and less experienced pupils.

Within the small group more pupils can contribute than if the discussion was with the whole class, and they can try out one or two ideas in their own language, come to some agreement, and support each other in pressing for their ideas to be adopted.

John's skills are in establishing the routines and in deciding for each occasion on the agendas and the time limits, which will be determined by the topic under discussion and by the mood of the form.

Finally, each group is expected to have an outcome from their discussions which will be shared with the whole form. This gives public recognition to their ideas and allows them to be seen as valuable and contributing to the end product. John's skills at this point, when he – rather than Sandra for example – is running the session, are basic teaching skills, accepting and acknowledging information and opinions, helping each group to express its ideas and helping the whole form to come to its own decisions or conclusions.

With those skills and strategies in mind let us put the course supervision session in Period 2 aside for the moment and examine the Physics lesson with a Year 10 group in Periods 3 and 4.

The **content** of the lesson was an experiment to investigate the moment of forces.

John began by asking one of the pupils to hold the end of a long pole – in fact a window pole – and to hold the pole out horizontally. Near the pupil's hands he hooked on a heavy weight. With the weight in this position the pupil was able to keep the pole horizontal, but as John moved the weight further along the end of the pole dipped. He demonstrated this again with one or two other pupils, showing how much more difficult it was to maintain the horizontal position as the weight neared the further end.

He then divided the class into their standard working groups of three, giving each group a metre rule and stand on which to balance it, two hooked weights and a selection of weights which fitted on to the hooks. He asked them to place a weight in any position on one end of the rule and to find out what weight, placed in which position on the other end of the rule, would balance it. They had to repeat this ten times, with differing weights at different distances from the point of balance, and to record the weights and distances which balanced each time. If different weights were used either side of the point of balance what happened to the distances? At the end of the experiment they looked for any pattern which emerged from their results.

After 35 minutes John stopped the work, collected the results on an overhead projector and asked what patterns had been noticed. A discussion took place with a little guidance, from which, as John had planned and hoped, the elements of the Law of Moments of Forces emerged. The final stage was for each group of three to return to their own results and compare their findings with the now established Law.

While the content of the lesson is new to the class the process – of working in groups, arriving at agreed conclusions in those groups, pooling information and sharing and discussing those conclusions with the whole class – is standard procedure to them, as it is to many pupils throughout the country involved in what is now being called 'Process Science'.

The lesson can be divided into three parts. In the first part, while John is demonstrating with the long pole and heavy weights the class are watching, but are also thinking as individuals about what they are seeing. The individual impressions, ideas and part-formed conclusions from that demonstration will be what each pupil brings to the second part of the lesson, the actual experiment in the group of three. These ideas will be shared, altered and confirmed by discussion during the experiment. In the third part the class pools and explores as a whole group the conclusions from each threesome. The fact that the experiments have been repeated some 80–100 times within the large group adds weight to any conclusions drawn.

The strategy used in the lesson is precisely that used in the form meeting – a movement from individual thought and response to work within the small group, and then to a sharing and pooling of ideas in the whole group; but these are not the only parallels between the two sessions. As before, the responsibility for the outcome of the lesson is placed firmly on the pupils: 'You have done this work – here are your results – what conclusions can you draw from them?' John's position once more is that of guide or consultant, with his authority accepted because of his greater knowledge.

In a further similarity between the two sessions, at the beginning of the third part of the Physics lesson John asked for the results from each group of three, and later for their observations of any patterns. Some of the results at least may have been wildly inaccurate because of carelessness, inability to read the rule properly and a dozen other reasons. But, as in the form meeting, the results offered have to be accepted and respected if further discussion is to take place freely. Critical comment too early would again be inappropriate and non-productive, but this does not mean that individual results cannot be later examined in the light of the patterns and rules formed by combining the class results. Once more then, there is initial uncritical acceptance so that ideas can come freely, followed by analysis in which individuals can compare their ideas for themselves with the framework created by the whole group.

The boundaries in this session are those enforced by the process of the experiment as well, of course, as those of classroom norms of behaviour. Within those boundaries, there is some freedom – to work through the set tasks in different ways, for example – and space for individual thought, action and effort.

Finally, even though the planned outcome of the lesson is increased knowledge about one aspect of physics, social skills are learned or reinforced also. To get good results each pupil must not only work as accurately as possible but must learn to trust the others in the group, and co-operate with them; they must learn to tolerate disagreement and work at resolving it.

Within the framework of John's Physics lesson therefore, as in his form period, at least three of the four conditions listed at the end of Chapter 5 are also met; there is respectful and accepting treatment of the class, boundaries are established and there is freedom, of action and decision, within them. There is obviously the chance also of repeated small successes, while failure is not emphasised or necessarily made public. It is clear from this that the 'central purpose of education' (HMI 1979), which we suggested in Chapter 5 was the main task of the form tutor – the personal and social development of the pupils in their form, with its emphasis on increased responsibility and a positive self-concept – can equally be furthered in the academic lesson, and indeed forms a foundation for confidence in academic work. Subjects such as English, the Humanities and Social Education have long recognised this potential and have, over the years, developed a range of classroom strategies and teaching methods appropriate to those ends. Other subjects – Maths, Languages and the Sciences, have more recently moved in a similar direction.

What the two sessions also have in common are the skills the member of staff uses. Of course there are differences in content and in emphasis; but the basic teaching skills, the skills which manage and engineer the process of learning for the pupils, are essentially the same for each. John Rivers has not had to put on a different hat, or be one person with one set of skills as a tutor and another person as a Physics teacher. The skills, values and attitudes to pupils valid for one situation are equally applicable in the other since his job is the same in each – the personal (including academic) and social development of the group of pupils.

Those skills of working with a large group – in the tutor period or the Physics lesson – are not the only ones the tutor and the subject teacher must develop in common. A further movement we have seen, in the late 1980s and early 1990s, is in the increased emphasis on one-to-one work with pupils, demanded by profiling, records of achievement, 'Review and Guidance', and course supervision in TVE and GCSE. This has affected both the subject teacher and the tutor, since the need is for individual guidance within each subject as well as for overall guidance. So the one-to-one skills that were traditionally demanded of the form tutor are now required equally by the subject teacher.

The same principles are applied in this one-to-one work as in the form period and the Physics lesson described above. 'Guidance interviews' – whatever their titles in a particular school – are at their best based on 'respectful, accepting and concerned treatment by "significant others".' Within them boundaries are set, freedom of decision and action is allowed within those boundaries and success is emphasised. As teachers become more confident, trained and skilled in one-to-one work, 'guidance interviews' will play an increasing part in promoting the 'personal and social development' of all pupils.

In the next chapter we examine some possible strategies and structures for such interviews, and show how the same strategies can be used in a 'guidance interview', in a helping interview with a pupil in distress and with a pupil in trouble for disruptive behaviour.

7
Individual Pupils

Period 2

In John's school, in Years 10 and 11, tutors are required to discuss with each pupil, at least twice each term, the work they are doing and the progress they are making. The school's name for this process is Course Supervision and the intention over the next few years is to extend this downwards so that all pupils eventually receive this guidance from Year 7. Staffing ratios in this authority have been adjusted recently to allow for the allocation of two periods each week of supervision time for pupils in Years 10 and 11 and one period each week in the lower school.

Course supervision was established in the school with three main functions.

1 Evaluative

- of how each pupil is coping with the work
- of how the work load is perceived by the pupils
- of how much the pupils understand of the school's work plans and coursework schedules, and of what the school expects of them
- of whether the demands of the workload and schedules are realistic; whether the pupils are able to cope with them; whether they work.

2 Preventative

In the sense that difficulties individual pupils might have in coping with the work levels and loads will be spotted early, and that last-minute panics for work to be handed in might be avoided.

To support and encourage. To help the pupils to a realistic self-appraisal of their work, to create positive strategies for working and learning and to an increasing assumption of active responsibility for their own work schedules and performances.

The aims listed above are specific to the academic aspects of school. But the means by which those aims are to be achieved – one-to-one discussions, a building of trust and a creation of rapport between the tutor and pupil – can be described as pastoral aims, demanding pastoral skills. In the process of course supervision therefore, the academic and pastoral divisions of the school come together. In addition, while the process of course supervision is focused on academic work, there is the hope that such trust and rapport will be of use when situations occur which are not concerned with academic work but with the wider aspects of the pupils' lives. It is also possible, and to be hoped, that the new relationships created in those interviews – conducted by subject teachers as well as by form tutors – will spill over into the working relationships in the classroom and around the school.

The difference these new relationships will make must not be underestimated. For the first time, for example, words such as 'negotiation' are being used to describe transactions between teachers – or tutors – and pupils. For the first time it is prescribed that pupils are to be treated as partners in an educational endeavour and, if 'negotiate' means anything, as partners with the right and power to bargain and have a legitimate say. There is nothing new here of course except the prescription – Profiling and Records of Achievement schemes have been using such concepts for years. But in many areas and schools these movements have been seen as extentions of pastoral work, and frequently have been used only with the less academically able. For the first time such concepts are applied to all pupils and are seen as essential to the central academic function of the school.

The school does not yet make use of profiling, or records of achievement, but will shortly be involved in the final extension phase of TVE. The interviewing techniques involved in course supervision are obviously similar to those demanded by profiling and will be directly useful in the 'review and guidance' procedures of TVE.

There were three people John wanted to see in this period; two, Harjit P and Alan O, as part of the normal sequence of course supervision and one, Martin W, who had seemed in difficulties when seen two weeks ago, and who needed a further check. Much of the preliminary work for the session had been done. John had talked to all three individually in tutor time and for this, their third supervision session, they should have done the rounds of their subject teachers and collected comments from them which they had discussed and agreed to before they were written down. The pupils have the responsibility, therefore, of initiating discussion with their subject teachers on their work and progress at least once in each term from the Christmas of Year 10.

As the form left the room at the end of the tutor period John reminded the three that they were to be seen that period and Harjit stayed behind. John placed himself at the end of the bench at which he was sitting, so that the corner of the bench was between them. There were reasons for this; he had found, when talking to individual pupils, that for him to sit behind his desk made the interview feel too formal, with the desk acting as a barrier, but that sitting at right angles to them with the token barrier of the corner of a desk, or in this case the corner of the bench between them, seemed to make the pupil feel more at ease then sitting side by side or face to face with nothing in between.

This is John's third supervision session with Harjit, but the first full review in which comments from all his subject teachers have been collected. In the previous two sessions they have discussed briefly his future plans, the things that interest him in and out of school, his work in, and feelings about, different subjects, the support he gets from parents and his working conditions at home. John has been careful not to be intrusive, to focus their discussions on school and work, and to talk about home or out-of-school matters only when Harjit has raised the topics, but nevertheless he has built a picture for himself, if only an initial and superficial one, of a warm and caring family life and a secure and happy environment. The results of John's careful 'partnership' approach can already be seen in Harjit's confidence and relaxed manner when talking with him.

Harjit himself is a bright and capable boy, likely to get good grades in most of his subjects, who expects to go on to the local Sixth Form College to do 'A' levels. In this he has the full support of his parents. There is, after one term in Year 10 however, a general feeling among the staff that Harjit needs some pressure to get him to produce work, and John knows that the comments on his report slips are likely to refer to his inability to hand in work on time, partly at least because of what many staff see as an over-active social life. This information is at the back of John's mind and sharing it could be part of his 'agenda' for the interview. He does not necessarily see it as his function, however, to reinforce the message if Harjit has, as is likely, already received it from his subject teachers. John's intention is to listen to Harjit's reaction to the review, to explore with him his perceptions of his work and progress, and to decide with him any action to be taken. Harjit is coming to the interview after a round of brief sessions with his subject teachers. He knows that the main purpose of the interview is to talk about his work, but John needs to be sensitive to any other 'agenda' Harjit might have for the meeting, which could well include a reference to the review comments on his social life.

As John sits down Harjit passes over the bundle of comment slips he has collected from his subject teachers.

John   Thanks. (*He smiles at him*) Hallo again. (*He waves the bundle of slips*) You've managed to get round everyone?

Harjit Yes sir.

John Good ... Well ... this session is going to be about the review of work you've just had, but I'd rather put these (*indicating the slips of paper*) on one side – we can come back to them later if we need them – and talk about how you feel about what was said. Is that OK with you?

Harjit Yes ... yes I think so.

(John is intent on putting the slips to one side here, because he wants Harjit's opinions and feelings. His question 'Is that OK with you?' obviously expects the answer 'Yes'. He misses or ignores the implications of the slight hesitancy on Harjit's part.)

John OK. (*He puts the slips to one side between them*) So ... are you happy with what was said – was it good?

Harjit Well ... it was quite good I suppose ... on the whole.

John (*nodding in agreement*) Mmm.

Harjit I mean I've had some good marks, especially in English and Social Studies, and none of the marks have been very poor. Most people seem to think I can get good grades. (*There is a slight emphasis on the 'can' and his voice is a little hesitant. John picks this up.*)

John From the way you say that there's a 'but' at the end of it.

Harjit Well, as I said, my marks are OK, on the whole, but I think there's too much work to do. In English for example, before we've finished one piece he's giving us another.

John You think there's too much work?

(John is reflecting back, in a neutral tone, what he understands Harjit to have said.)

Harjit Yes – and I'm not the only one. I mean there's always something waiting, and we're usually handing it in a few days late.

John But it worries you when you're late?

(John ignores Harjit's effort to be seen as only one of many and makes his comment specific to him.)

Harjit Yes ... it does. I don't like being told off for being behind and I don't like the feeling of never being able to catch up.

John It feels impossible to catch up?

Harjit If it would only stop for a moment I could. I've almost finished last weekend's homework but he gave us a description piece in class on Monday that he wanted finished for today. I should be able to finish them both over the weekend, but he is likely to set us another piece today and then I'll be behind again.

John Hmmm ... so even though your marks have been pretty good you feel there's a lot to do in English, and you're handing work in late each time – even if it's only a few days late. This worries you, because you don't like being told off, and you don't like the pressure, the feeling of never catching up. Is that right?

Harjit Yes, (*he smiles a little*) I suppose that sums it up.

John OK. Well ... I think there are things we can do to help you sort it out, but before going on to those can I ask you about the other subjects? Does the same thing happen with them?

(For the most part John has been making statements to Harjit which reflect back to him the things he has said, and what he understands to be his feelings about the work situation, in order to get him to expand and explore his initial statements. In his last comments he summarises what he has said so far to ensure that they have a common understanding. This will help Harjit to clarify his feelings about what has happened and give him a chance to correct any wrong impressions John has picked up. John is also mentioning action – positive steps to help – that he and Harjit can take together. At this point in the interview it is important that Harjit knows there are things that can be done, that having discussed his difficulty action can be taken, but it is also important that the actions are seen to be joint ones; that Harjit will be involved in them and take some responsibility.)

Harjit Not to the same extent. English is mostly course work so there's more to do in that. But there's homework set in some subjects and pieces of course work in others that you have weeks to do, then suddenly everyone seems to be asking for things at once.

John So work from other subjects piles up as well.

Harjit Well, it's not just that it piles up but it all comes at once. Look at last week for example. (*His voice goes up a little in pitch and his hand movements become stronger*) I had one piece of English left over from the week before, then he gave us another piece, then we had a Social Studies essay to do for Mrs Samson – she wanted that in by Thursday as well, then there was homework from Maths, Chemistry and Biology and ... French. I'm supposed to be getting on with my CDT study and I haven't touched that for weeks. For Geography we've got to write something about the town for next week and that means talking to people and going to the library. There's hours of work even before I write anything. It all comes at once, as if none of the teachers know what the others are doing.

John (*pausing for a moment*) Hmm ... and that feels like a lot of pressure. It also makes you angry doesn't it?

(John's pause is quite deliberate after Harjit's long and vehement speech.)

Harjit Well it does. (*His manner becomes calmer after John's pause and acceptance of his feelings*) I think it ought to be organised so that the work comes at a steady rate, not all at once. It's supposed to be isn't it? When it isn't no-one can cope with it.

John Hmm ... I think I'd like to ask around about last week and find out what happened. You're right, we do have work schedules and what you describe ought not to happen – or at least not happen too often. Was that the worst week you've had so far, for things coming all at once?

Harjit No, there was one week just before Christmas when everybody seemed to be saying they definitely wanted things done before the holidays. It was as if the teachers were fighting each other to see who could get their work in first. I started about four different subjects but they all had to be in by the end of the week. That's crazy isn't it?

John It sounds impossible. I'll ask how that week came about and come back to you. How did you manage with the sudden rush?

Harjit In the end I gave up.

John You gave up. (*This is a flat reflection of what Harjit has said, not a question implying that he shouldn't have done.*)

Harjit If I was going to have three rows I thought I might just as well have a fourth – so I went out with my girlfriend to a party.

(Harjit laughed when he said this, but the words came over defiantly. This is the first indication of the comments John has heard about Harjit from other staff. He wants to acknowledge what has been said, and to recognise the defiance, but is hesitant about jumping straight at it.)

John Did you indeed! (*smiling in response to Harjit's laugh*) That's still Joanna isn't it? Did you decide together to say to hell with it?

Harjit No. She'd finished and handed in all her work by then. But she doesn't seem to have the same sort of pressure in Year 11.

John Is that what she says?

Harjit No, she says it gets worse, but I don't think it can do. She seems to manage to get much more time for other things – she can even help me with my homework sometimes. Although we only go out about once a week if that's what you're thinking. (*Harjit's head came up*)

(John had moved slightly sideways from the subject of Harjit's social life but obviously Harjit had this topic as a part of his 'agenda', and came straight back to it. Each mention he made of it had a level of challenge in it, and John had to pick it up straight this time. This is probably the reason also for Harjit's hesitation at the beginning – there were remarks on the report slips he wants to discuss.)

John You mean I could be thinking that you go out too often?

Harjit Well one or two of the teachers have made comments about having to be careful not to let 'my social life' (*imitating another accent*) interfere with my work. (*bitterly*)

John That's made you angry as well.

(John picks up the feeling and reflects it back to him)

Harjit Yes it does. I'm not going to stop seeing her. And I can't stop in and do homework every night – I should go crazy.

John	Yes I think you probably would. Is that what's being suggested?
Harjit	(*still bitterly*) I think that's what they'd like to happen. They've put comments about 'my social life' on my report slips as well so my father and mother will see them.
John	So there's probably going to be trouble at home. What do you think your parents will do about it?
Harjit	Well they'll start worrying and probably stop me from going round to Joanna's in the week or her coming round to my place. But in the week we don't see each other 'till about nine o'clock or half past nine. If I've still got work to do I take it round and she helps me with it if its one of her subjects, so it doesn't interfere with work – it helps it. (*emphatically*)
John	(*pauses for a moment*) You believe it helps your work.

(This is not a question but a straight reflection back of what Harjit has said, stated without disbelief. The result is that Harjit has to think about whether he really believes it or is being defensive.)

Harjit	(*smiles and relaxes a little*) Sometimes she has been able to help me with things; but I've usually finished for the night when we meet – and we don't meet every night.
John	OK – so you're going to try to persuade your parents that Joanna coming round to you – or you going to Joanna's – doesn't stop you working. Are you certain yourself that it doesn't?
Harjit	Yes. I think she helps me and encourages me ... and if I've got to finish something she sits with me while I do it or helps me.
John	So it doesn't get in the way at all.
Harjit	No I don't think it does – oh I suppose sometimes I've left something unfinished to go round, or stopped before she comes when I've still got work to do, but not very often.
John	So you think the staff comments might cause a difficulty with your parents. You want to go on seeing Joanna; they might want to stop you meeting altogether in the week. Perhaps you need to think of a compromise – make some nights definitely clear, for example.
Harjit	We don't meet every night even now. This week, for example, I went round to her place on Monday and Joanna came round home on Thursday. (*pause*) Do you think it's a bad thing then? (*accusingly*)
John	From what you've said it sometimes stops you from working. It depends how often that happens doesn't it? You're the only one who really knows.
Harjit	It doesn't always happen. (*forcefully*)
John	This is a pretty touchy subject for you isn't it? It feels as if you're practising on me what you're going to say to your parents.
Harjit	Yes, but they might ask you what you think, at the next parents' evening.
John	Yes they might, mightn't they? And at the moment I wouldn't

	know what to say, except that there's obviously something going wrong. But I wouldn't have said it's just meeting Joanna.
Harjit	What do you mean?
John	Well, let's have a look at what we've said so far, because I think we need to move on to what we do about it. You've said your marks are good, on the whole, but you get behind with your work a bit, particularly in English, and you're finding that you never really have time to catch up. People have been telling you off about this and you don't like it. But you feel there's too much work and that things ought to be more organised so that a lot of work isn't pushed at you suddenly. You feel there's too much pressure, because of the amount of work set and the way all your teachers expect their work to be done on the date they set, regardless of any other work. Yes?
Harjit	Yes, that's right. (*with feeling*)
John	Because you said that, I've promised to ask about what happened last week, when you seemed to have a lot of work all at once, and about the week before Christmas, when the same thing happened. But I've also said that we should look for ways of helping you to manage your work better, OK?
Harjit	Yes.
John	The other side to this is that some of your teachers, since your work is being handed in late, have suggested that you and Joanna see too much of each other. You're annoyed about this and especially that what they said has been written down and will go to your parents. Right?

(John is again summing up what has been said, and reflecting back to Harjit not only facts but his understanding of Harjit's feelings about the situation, based as much on facial expression, tone of voice and posture as on the words he has used. Even if John has interpreted Harjit's feelings wrongly, and they were very clear in this case, this does not matter as long as Harjit feels he has the right to disagree with what has been said. This too will help Harjit to clarify his own understanding, and places his feelings 'on the agenda' so that they can be considered and discussed.)

Harjit	Well ... yes ... I am fed up about it. I mean ... what I do in the evenings is my business. It just seems that school work is taking over and interfering in everything, as if there shouldn't be anything else.
John	Mmm ... I can see you feel that. In fact I got the idea earlier that when each new piece of work is set it comes as a surprise – a nasty shock – to you, and that you resent it, as if the teacher is setting it to get at you and stop you doing other things. Is that a fair comment?
Harjit	Well ... no, it's not as bad as that. (*smiling*) I mean I know in one way that there's going to be an essay each week, and more coming from other subjects. I suppose I resent it because it means I can't do anything else ... and it never seems to stop. I work at one

piece and finish it and think 'Good, that's that done', but before I've had time to catch my breath I'm in the middle of another one and someone else is telling me off because their's is late.

John So at the moment it's as if there's too much work, a struggle to get things in on time, never really succeeding and always being in trouble and being told off. Like running very hard to stay on the same spot.

(In his last two comments John is again feeding back to Harjit impressions and feelings, exaggerating a little to make them clearer, and using different words to present them to him.)

Harjit Yes. That's it exactly. (*smiling again*) And what worries me most is that we're only at the beginning of the course. If this goes on for another year and a half I shall go mad.

(Harjit began the interview feeling a little bruised by the review process, but the defensiveness there at the start has mostly disappeared. This is largely due to the fact that John has not been critical about his late work, and to the understanding comments made about his feelings and reactions. In no sense has John agreed that there is too much work, or that Harjit's teachers are behaving unreasonably in setting it, although he is aware that, even with the schools organised work schedules, demands from the teachers can become irrational and conflicting at times. He is also aware that Harjit is not coping particularly well with his efforts to maintain both work and play, and that some of his statements are a projection of his feelings of chaos on to his teachers – it is they who are disorganised, not himself. He has promised to investigate what the school has done but he has also made it clear that Harjit must do something as well. Showing some understanding of Harjit's feelings allowed him to move on from them and gives John a chance to talk with him more freely about the amount of time that has to be given to the work and to suggest strategies for using his time productively.)

John Hmm ... (*smiling back*) As I said, it's fairly obvious something's got to happen – so if you're going to go mad if this goes on have you thought of what might change?

Harjit Well, as I said before I think it would help if the work was more organised and more regular. But the only other thing I can think of is if I drop one of my subjects. I know I can't drop Maths, which is my weakest subject, but I could drop Geography and I don't really need two Sciences. I think then I should have more time for the others.

John OK ... so dropping a subject is one possibility. Any other ideas?

(This is not something the school would find acceptable from someone with Harjit's ability at this stage in the course. Nevertheless, John makes no comment about it but accepts it as one idea – and asks for others.)

Harjit	Well no ... I think the real problem is there's too much work.
John	Is there anything you think you can do yourself? (*pauses for a moment*) I'll tell you why I asked that. Both the ideas you've suggested mean changing what's coming to you from outside – the school gets more organised and the work comes more regularly – and I hope they do – and you drop a subject to give you more time. But what that says is 'it's all them – not me. They've got to change, I don't need to'. Do you see what I mean?
Harjit	I hadn't thought of it like that.
John	I think it's easier to see from outside. But there is a point there isn't there?
Harjit	Well ... yes.
John	OK, so I wonder about how you manage things – and what could change there. First I wonder how you use the time you've got. I don't mean going round to Joanna's or going out – I mean everyday time, how you plan your evenings, what you do when you come in from school. Second, and this comes later perhaps, I wonder how you plan your work and if better planning wouldn't help. I mean – we're not talking about a disaster over that last term are we? We're talking about an intelligent and capable person who's a bit behind with their work and feels under pressure.
Harjit	It seems like a disaster at times.
John	Mmm ... I'm sure it does, particularly after this review – which wasn't as good as you hoped. But I think the first place to look is at your own organisation. I'd like to make a suggestion which I think might help you organise yourself. Do you want to try?
Harjit	Well – I don't know what you want.
John	If I asked you what you did in the evenings what would you say?
Harjit	That's easy – homework and then more homework.
John	OK ... but in fact you do a lot of other things as well don't you – eat, sleep, relax, play music, watch television, talk. Do your evenings have a regular pattern?
Harjit	I don't know what you mean.
John	Well – do you always go to bed at the same time, or have your tea at the same time each evening, or watch any particular television programmes?
Harjit	There are some television programmes that I like to watch – and we always have tea at about five o'clock.
John	So there's some events and some regular spaces. What time do you usually get in from school?
Harjit	Somewhere between four o'clock and quarter past on most days. Sometimes a bit later, and I stay behind on Wednesdays for Drama Club.
John	So let's say 'after school' starts at half past four. What I suggest you do is keep a note, a sort of log book, over the next two weeks, of what you do in the evenings. Write it up each night before you go to bed.
Harjit	What sort of thing would I write?

(John is pushing the idea a bit, since he wants to have some positive outcome and time is getting on. Harjit obviously feels a little pushed over the last few minutes and, sensibly, is reluctant to commit himself without understanding. The fact that he feels able to ask for clarification in this way is an indication of John's success in working with him.)

John   Have a look at these – they might explain it and might make it easier. (*Goes over to his desk and takes some sheets of paper from a drawer*) They're just printed sheets with times written on each half hour. I know they begin at four o'clock but ignore the first half hour. Then against each time you write what you were doing then. 5.00 – Tea, for example, or 5.30 – Neighbours. 7.30 – English homework, 8.30 – still English homework, 11.30 – French.

Harjit   Oh ... I see, like a diary.

John   Yes that's right – like a diary. The idea is that you find out what it is you do with your time, how much you spend on one thing, how much on another. When you've done that you'll find it easier to decide how much time you want to spend on something – in other words, it might help you to manage it better.

    I don't necessarily want to see these – like a diary, what you put on them belongs to you – but I would like to talk with you for a few minutes in two weeks' time about what you've found – any ideas you've got then for using the time better, any gaps you find. Are you willing to have a go?

Harjit   Well I can see it might be useful. I've often wondered where the time goes. (*smiling*)

John   OK ... I think then we can look at the second part – how you plan and organise your work – if we know what time you've got. All clear?

Harjit   Yes I think so.

John   I'll see you in a fortnight then. I've put it in my diary and I'll remind you on the day. OK?

Harjit   Alright sir. Thank you. (*Harjit leaves the room*)

John made a note of what he had asked Harjit to do and then went to find Alan O.

Perhaps we should make it clear that the session with Harjit is not intended to show a perfect interview, nor John as the perfect interviewer. Indeed there is probably no such thing as the perfect interview. We chose Harjit as an example because he is, of course, a good interviewee. He is intelligent and articulate and because of his repeated successes in school work over the previous years, and his intention to go on with it, he is obviously not alienated from the ideals of school nor particularly apprehensive of 'an interview'. He is probably, in this, a fair representative of the majority of Year 10 and 11 pupils in the majority of schools. An example of a session with someone who could or would not talk, who resented the whole system, or who had no wish to take part in school processes would not have illustrated the points we wished to make.

The first of these points is that John tries to start the interview from 'where the pupil is', with Harjit's own thoughts, feelings and reactions, rather than from a statement of the views and positions of his teachers. He felt the place for that was later, when Harjit's own views and positions have been explored and respected.

In fact, as became obvious, Harjit had an 'agenda' in which discussion of the comments written by his subject teachers was a priority. Although John missed the first indications of this, when he did become aware of Harjit's 'agenda' it was recognised and accepted.

The second point is that the interview has a shape, a pattern, which is structured and intentional. John begins by *listening* rather than telling and *reflecting* back to Harjit the things he has said. Later on John *summarises* what he believes has been said, and also *reflects* back to Harjit what has been said and what he is picking up about Harjit's feelings. The interview ends with something positive: a plan for *action*, which in this case means monitoring time for two weeks but which might only have been, for example, a reference to the scheduled repeat interview in March. So the pattern of the interview, based on the three stage model suggested by Egan (1975) for the 'skilled helper', is that of first, listening and exploring; second, clarifying and expanding the understanding of both parties and third, taking mutually agreed action and decisions.

The skills involved for the tutor are those highlighted in the previous paragraph – those of listening, reflecting and summarising. In addition the tutor needs flexibility and a range of strategies for action which are consonant with the overall aims of the supervision – the increase in responsibility for the work by the pupil.

Fundamental to this interview also, and to those that follow, is John's adherence to the four basic conditions of positive and effective tutor/pupil and teacher/pupil relationships discussed in Chapter 5 and illustrated in action in the large group work in Chapter 6. John shows his concern, he listens with respect, and accepts the person, if not always the things, that are said. As we pointed out in Chapter 5 he cannot make himself 'significant' to Harjit – only Harjit himself can select John for that position – but John at least offers the contact and shows the concern and positive feelings which could make his selection possible.

In the interview boundaries are evident: in the language used between the two, in the acceptance of John's authority and the acceptance of the purpose and framework of the interview. Within that framework Harjit has freedom of expression and, to a degree, freedom of action. His commitment to keeping the record of evening activity has to come voluntarily and, while he is pushed a little, no decisions are made for him. The whole process is aimed not just at increasing the chances of his success in academic work but in enabling him to increase control over his activities.

There are therefore two complementary aspects to the interview. The first is the framework of the tutor/pupil relationship, in which the aim is the increase in the pupil's responsibility, personal power and positive self-concept and which observes the four conditions for such a relationship discussed earlier. The second is the pattern of the 3-stage model, which in effect says 'Where are you now? Where do you want to get to? What do you have to do to get there?', which uses the listening skills of reflection and summarising to help the pupil explore each of those areas and which ends with an agreed plan of action.

John's session in Period 5, an interview with a pupil in his form who has asked for time to talk about a difficulty she is experiencing, illustrates the use of similar skills and strategies in a different context.

Period 5
John filled in the register for his form after lunch and sent them off to their lesson. As they moved out Marie L stayed behind, having already asked permission of her teacher for that lesson to see Mr Rivers. John asked Marie to sit down and then placed himself, as he had with Harjit, at the end of the bench at which she was sitting, so that the corner of the bench came between them.

Marie sat with her head bent, staring at the bench top, her fingers playing with the school bag before her and saying nothing. After a while John began.

John Is it hard to begin?

(John is leaving the initiative with Marie, and his words are framed as encouragement. There was an initial silence while Marie sat but if that went on too long Marie would find it increasingly difficult to start. So John speaks to break the silence.)
(Marie looks up for a moment and then down again)

Marie Sir ... I wanted to see you because I want to change classes.

(There is a pause while John gives Marie time to go on)

John I see. That seems quite a big step. (*John pauses*) Look, Marie, I have noticed that you've been sitting on your own recently, and not looking happy about it. Can you tell me what's happened?

(The phrasing here is important, particularly at this stage of the interview. John has indicated that he recognises her feelings, and that may allow them to be talked about, but he is also indicating, by the way he puts his question, that Marie can choose what she tells him – he is not making demands.)

Marie Well ... I used to be friends with Denise and Mandy. (*Marie is still looking down at the bench*) Denise and I have been friends

since we started school. But I had an argument with her over . . .
over something she said . . . so we're not friends any more and
that means I haven't any friends in this class.

John   What about Mandy?

Marie   Mandy's taken Denise's side and she's going round telling lies
about me and stirring all the others up against me.

John   And that's upsetting you?

Marie   Yes. (*Marie's head lifted and her voice became stronger.*) Mandy
says it's all my fault that Denise and me had a row, and that I
called her names and she was only trying to be helpful.

John   What does Denise say?

Marie   Denise doesn't say anything but she won't talk to me. Mandy's
got all the others not talking to me. They just talk about me as if I
wasn't there.

John   What you're saying is that you had an argument with Denise
when she said something to upset you. You got angry and called
her names so she and Mandy aren't friends with you now and
they're not talking to you. At the moment you feel very much on
your own and that everyone else is against you?

Marie nodded.

(John is reviewing what has been said so far, to give them a point of
agreement from which they can move on, and is also demonstrating some
understanding of Marie's feelings. He also has a decision to make here. It
is obvious that what Denise said to Marie touched on a sensitive area.
John has no idea what this might be, and Marie has not yet given him the
information. He could ignore that aspect and concentrate on the problem
that is being presented – that of the breakdown of the friendship. Or he
could ask if Marie will tell him what the quarrel was about and concentrate on that aspect of the situation. Because Marie has seemed miserable
for some time he decides to do the latter, but again, both the phrasing and
the tone of voice he uses give her the choice of answering it.)

John   The argument must have been about something that mattered a
lot, Marie. Can you tell me what it was?

Marie   (*dropping her eyes again*) I . . . well . . . she said something about
my mother . . .

(John sits still in silence for a moment and then speaks quietly.)

John   Something that upset you?

Marie   She . . . she asked me if it was true that Mum was going out with
someone else. (*Marie paused again*)

John   Mmm?

Marie   She said someone had seen her. She wanted to know if it was true
that Dad was moving out – that they were going to get divorced.

(Marie's head is still bowed and John can see tears on her cheeks. Again there is a pause.)

John   That must have hurt you. I can understand you getting angry.

Marie   *(lifting her head a little)* I yelled at her and called her names. I told her she had no right to go around saying things like that.

(Another silence)

John   And then?

Marie   *(crying openly now)* She walked off.

(John has another decision to make here. From Marie's reaction it is likely that Denise's question hit on what are at least Marie's fears and anxieties, even if she has no certain knowledge of her parent's situation or intentions. To some degree she is denying even to herself what she may well know. John could probably get Marie to discuss her fears or knowledge, and at some point, though not necessarily with him, this may well be necessary, to help her to come to terms with what may well be the reality of a parental break-up. But Marie is not asking for that, and John is not certain of his ability to handle the situation if she did. The problem she is presenting to him is about the relationship between herself and Denise, and her distress over the breaking of that friendship. John feels that if her parents are in the process of separating Marie needs the support of a long-term friend like Denise and decides for the moment therefore to concentrate on the situation between herself and Denise and the other girls in the class. He accepts Marie's distress without comment and without trying to stop the flood of tears. After a while Marie dries her eyes but remains with her eyes on the bench.)

John   *(quietly)* Marie – it seems to me that the reason you're upset is because Denise walked off and won't talk to you now. Is that right?

(Marie nods her head.)

John   I'd like you to think about this for a moment. Do you think Denise was trying to hurt you by talking about your Mum and Dad? Did she want to upset you?

Marie   I . . . I don't know.

John   Well, let me make a guess. Denise asked you, when just the two of you were together, if this story about your Mum and Dad was true. The idea upset you, so you got angry with her, then she got upset because you were calling her names and walked off. Is that roughly what happened?

Marie   Yes. *(Marie's eyes are still on the bench in front of her.)*

(It seems to John that Marie has got herself trapped by her own hurt reaction to Denise's question, and that she needs help to get out of that trap. Her defence against the other girls' attacks has been to blame Denise, and before she can take action she must examine her own responsibility in what happened. So John is pushing her a little by confronting her with a different interpretation and a chance to move away from the stalemate.)

John   (*pauses for a moment*) Do you wish you hadn't got angry?
(*Marie nods again.*)
John   (*pauses again*) OK ... so what you really want at the moment is to get back to being friends with Denise. Yes?
Marie She won't. (*Her head lifts*)
John   I asked about *you*. Is that what *you* want?
(*Marie nods*)
John   So somehow you've got to start talking to her.
Marie I don't think she will.
John   Let's go back to you again, and get it clear what you want. I know you've been hurt by the row with Denise, and by what the other girls have done. But you wish you hadn't got angry with Denise and you'd like to be friends with her again. Would *you* like to talk to *her*?

(John emphasises the 'you' in the last two sentences. He wants to keep the focus on Marie's feelings, not her defences against action with Denise. When faced with the stalemate Marie is creating he goes back to summarising the feelings that have been expressed.)

Marie (*mumbles*) Yes.
John   But you're a bit scared to try.
Marie I know she won't have anything to do with me.
John   I think this is where you're getting stuck. Because what you're saying is 'I want to talk to her but I'm not going to because I know she won't talk to me'.
Marie Well I know if I tried she'd walk away again.
John   She may do of course, because she's likely to be hurt and upset as well. I think you're scared of being hurt again, and I can understand that. Well – there seem to me to be three possibilities. One – we leave things as they are. Two – you try to talk to her over the next few days. Three – you get someone else, me for example or another friend of you both, to talk to her first.

(John summarises three possible courses of action.)

Marie How do you mean sir?
John   Well, if I were doing it I could find Denise and ask her if she would come with me to talk to you.
Marie Perhaps she wouldn't come.
John   Well ... I can't make her. Would you like me to try?
Marie I think so sir – but what would you say to her?
John   That depends on you. What would you like me to say to her?
Marie I don't know ... I think just that I want to talk to her, but when none of the other girls were around.

John	OK ... Can I tell her that you and I have talked about your argument and what caused it?
Marie	Yes, alright.
John	And you're happy for me to go ahead and ask her to come here?
Marie	(*Nods her head*) Mmm.
John	Do you want me there when you talk?
Marie	Mmm ... I think so.
John	OK ... I'll ask Denise if she wants that as well. If you both think it would be useful I'll sit in with you – and act as referee. You wait here while I go and find Denise and tell her what we've agreed that I can tell her. If she's happy to talk with you I'll bring her back now. Alright?
Marie	(*nods her head*)
John	One final point – I haven't forgotten your first suggestion that you change forms. But perhaps we try this with Denise first and then see how you feel, OK?
Marie	Yes sir.

(John leaves the room to find Denise.)

The context of this session with Marie is different, of course, from that of the one with Harjit. His was a prescribed part of the school procedures, Marie's was initiated by her – a request for help disguised at the beginning as a request to change forms. In another sense however, the interview with Marie was just as much a part of school procedures and just as much a part of the tutor's job.

The content of the interviews is again both different and alike. Harjit's was focused on academic work but involved a social difficulty as much as did Marie's. Fundamentally the situations are similar and the process of working is similar.

In each interview:

- the same techniques – of reflection, summarising and a suggested strategy for action were used
- a three stage process was observed – briefly, where are you now, where do you want to get to, how can you get there?
- the pupil was left with the responsibility and ultimately the power of making decisions – even if at times it was only to say yes or no to John's suggestions
- the pupil's privacy was respected
- feelings were recognised and accepted
- it was understood that feelings are powerful determinants of what happens and what can be done.

In each of these interviews John had adequate time and a degree of privacy. This is not always so of course, although time boundaries serve a vital purpose and, as Dr Johnson said of hanging, 'concentrate the mind wonderfully'. Both pupils came to the interview willingly and with something to say, and again this is not always so. Let us watch John dealing briefly with a disciplinary difficulty, and trying to observe the same principles as in his previous sessions.

Break Time
John waited in his room, after his Course Supervision session was over, for Darrel T to appear.

John Come in Darrel. Sit down. This isn't going to take long now but we need to start things moving. This hassle with Mr Davies. You were in trouble with him again in your last CDT lesson – is that right?

Darrel Er ... yes sir.

John From what Mr Davies tells me there has been quite a lot of trouble over the past few weeks, and this is the second time you've been in detention for playing around in his lesson. Yes?

Darrel Yes sir.

John Well, from what Mr Davies has said, it seems to me that the point's been reached where, unless something changes, you won't be allowed in the workshops. Has Mr Davies said that to you?

(Stage one – is this where you are?)

Darrel Yes sir, that's what he said.

John Since you opted for CDT in the first place, presumably you don't want to be kicked out of it?

Darrel Not really sir.

John Are you sure? You do really want to stay in there?

Darrel Yes sir.

(Stage two – is this where you want to get to?)

John OK – then the situation seems to me to be fairly simple. Mr Davies is angry, and fed up with what's been happening, and my guess is you're getting angry and fed up as well. You don't want to be thrown out of the workshop; Mr Davies says that unless something changes you will be. Does that sum things up?

Darrel Yes sir.

John Then I think you've got a job to do. Before the next CDT lesson you've got to find a way of stopping being thrown out altogether. Can you do that?

Darrel I don't know sir.

John Well – that's honest at least. But you also know it's got to be done. If you want, I'll try and help. Let's put it this way – I'm happy to help if you want to work at this, but I can't make you and I'm not going to try because that would be a waste of time. So ... do we have an agreement?

(John is making his own position clear and at the same time trying to get some commitment from Darrel.)

Darrel Yes I think so.

John Right – so here's the first of the bad news. You've got some homework. Over the weekend I want you to come up with a list of the things that need to change if you're not going to have any more rows with Mr Davies. I'll come up with some ideas as well. You write yours down, I'll write mine down, and on Monday, after school, we'll spend fifteen minutes comparing our lists and looking at how to put the changes into action. Is that acceptable?

(John is presenting stage three – the start of a plan for action)

Darrel Yes sir, I think so.

John And you can manage fifteen minutes after school on Monday?

(This is put as a question to Darrel to avoid the possibility of it being seen as another detention.)

Darrel Yes.

John OK. I'll be here with my list – see you then with yours.

(Darrel left the room and John went off to the staffroom for some coffee.)

John has used the brief interview to establish why they are meeting, an agreed contract and the hoped-for outcome. He deliberately keeps his voice at a matter-of-fact level, without any threatening, angry or unfriendly overtones. Darrel still feels defensive of course, because he knows this is a disciplinary situation, and his answers at first are brief, wooden and unresponsive.

John's message in the interview is a positive one. He makes it clear that he is not conducting an inquest on what happened and that he is not adding another punishment or a reprimand. Mr Davies has put Darrel in detention for his behaviour, he has been punished and the incident can legitimately be seen as closed. John also makes it clear that he wants to start from the situation now, and work towards avoiding such confrontations in the future. Any discussion of what happened in the CDT lesson will be diagnostic, not recriminatory, and John emphasises this by keeping a balance in the work to be done. He gives himself a task over the weekend to parallel Darrel's, and if the fifteen minutes on Monday is a detention then John is in there too.

If we go back to the list above, of strategies and principles drawn from the two previous interviews, it is clear that John still sticks fairly closely to most of them. He does little listening or reflecting – that may come in the session on Monday – but he certainly summarises the position as he understands it. Even with John doing most of the talking the interview follows the three-stage process, but in this instance becomes 'do you agree that this is where you are? Is this where you want to get to? OK then, here's what we do first'.

Darrel was left with the responsibility of making decisions about the agreement and about coming on Monday evening. This was not a false or a forced agreement – nor is it a final one. What John is trying to do, in a matter of fact manner, is to make Darrel aware of the consequences of doing nothing and to create space for a further meeting in which they can work together.

The issue of privacy did not arise, but Darrel's probable feelings of anger and resentment were recognised and accepted, and behind John's pressure to work towards a solution is his understanding that Darrel can become trapped in his own resentment and find it hard to think in positive terms of changes he might make. Once more three of the four conditions – concern, respect and acceptance, boundaries, and some freedom of choice within them – create the framework within which the interview takes place, and although the fourth, the chance of successes, cannot be guaranteed, observance of the other conditions at least gives it a chance.

In this and in the two previous chapters we have used the daily work of one particular tutor to illustrate a way of working with pupils, as a tutor or as a teacher, which enables pastoral – and hence educational – aims to be met; and we have examined John's teaching and tutoring work in some detail to show that model working in practice.

Because the model is one which can be applied to any 'helping relationship', it is possible for John to work with his form, with his Physics classes, or with individual pupils in this way, regardless of what is going on around him, or of other models of tutor/pupil relationships in use in the school. Fortunately for John however, he is not working in isolation. He also has the basic conditions necessary for his work to be properly effective, which in fact are the conditions the tutors we discussed in Chapter 4 were looking for, to enable them to do their job in the way they wished to do it.

John has been given, for example, a major responsibility for the welfare and discipline of 'his' pupils. He is able to work with confidence, with the assumption that a situation he is dealing with will not suddenly be taken out of his hands. He has time with his form, and time for one-to-one work on review and guidance. He works within a system which is based on a degree of tutor ascendancy, and feels supported in what he does by the context in which he works – the pastoral structure, the management processes and the expectations of those around him.

The link between the work of the tutor and the pastoral structure and processes which either enable or inhibit that work is a significant one. In Chapter 3 we described the 'real form tutors' we had met, and discussed how inadequately we felt the usual models of pastoral structures described their status and their relationships with pastoral Heads. We made the point also that the hierarchical nature of those structures and the 'passing on', 'referral upwards' processes implicit in them, militated against 'care', rein-forced the pastoral/academic divide and prevented the form tutor from doing his or her job. We described one model (that of the Biddick School), which placed tutoring at the centre of the school's activities, and suggested that this pointed the way to overcoming many of the problems created by the traditional Head of Year or House with tutors beneath them.

A number of the schools in which we discussed pastoral structures and the role of tutors with senior staff were in fact changing to move nearer to the 'Biddick' model, even as we communicated with them. In the next chapter we shall move away from John Rivers to examine the structural changes in two of those schools in some detail, the reasons given for the changes, and the implications of those changes for the relationships between tutors, their colleagues and their managers.

8
New Structures

Valley High School

Valley School has been both lucky and unlucky in the past year or so. Unlucky in that over the last two years much of the senior management team has changed and four of the Heads of Year have left. As in any school, their knowledge and experience are missed. What this has done, and this is the lucky part, is to make changes in structure and role not only easier but necessary.

Valley school had had a more or less orthodox system of Heads of Year working to a pastoral deputy, although, rather unusually, many of the Heads of Year also held other responsible positions. Inevitably over the course of a few years, as in many schools, 'pastoral care', administration and organisation, welfare, control and discipline, had come to be identified as the province of six or seven members of staff. Equally inevitably, many other members of staff had come to feel that the pastoral aspect of school did not concern them, while others, who were interested and wished to be involved, had come to feel that the pastoral team had established strongly defended territorial rights and resented them.

Change, then, was necessary and the chance to change was there. Over the course of a year or more, through a process of working together on Inset days and working parties, five teams of teachers have been created from groupings of academic subjects. The teams are not 'faculties'. Each subject retains its own Head of Department and its own autonomy; there is no overall team leader and the subjects grouped together are not necessarily those which could combine to form a faculty, nor are they intended to. The purpose of the groupings is purely pastoral, based on numbers of tutors and an appropriate mix. The groupings used are:

Team 1   Science and Home Economics
Team 2   Modern Languages and Business Studies
Team 3   PE, Music, Drama and Art
Team 4   Maths and Technology
Team 5   English and Humanities

Each of these five teams has pastoral responsibility for one 'Year' of the school, on a rotating basis, and makes up the team of tutors who take the forms of that Year. What the grouping of subjects does is give each team similar numbers of teachers and a useful variety of strengths. Each team has some 'floating' teachers who may not, at any one time, have a form but who provide support to the tutors, substitute when one is absent, and are equally involved in the PSE work of each Year.

From each of the teams a 'Pastoral Adviser' has been selected whose function is to 'service' the tutors in each team, to provide help and support for them in their task of tutoring and to co-ordinate their work. The Pastoral Advisers have a team-building and training function and are responsible for the induction of new staff. They are team leaders in the pastoral work of the team, but leaders in the *primus inter pares* sense – first among equals rather than Heads of Year; and they are, of course, members of one of the subject teams or departments that make up each team. Their positions are functions rather than posts, and their salaries vary, those who were on the Standard Scale being given an 'A' allowance for their work.

Finally, a Senior Pastoral Adviser was appointed to support the Year Advisers and to work closely with a Deputy who is responsible for both curriculum and pastoral work.

The Highlands School

Highlands School has also undergone many changes of staff over the last few years, but not specifically on the pastoral side. A core of people who held Head of Year positions remain in post, usually on a 'B' allowance, so the school is still able to use their experience and expertise. In spite of this the developments over the last two years at Highlands are in many ways more radical than those at Valley School, although there is a basic similarity, and have been to the management of the school rather than specifically to the pastoral structure. Subjects have been grouped to form, for the most part, coherent areas of curriculum experience. Each major subject area retains a 'Head of Department', on a B or C allowance, but each group of subjects has a 'Team Leader' on a D or E allowance with a management and co-ordinating function.

The groupings in Highlands School are:
1   Expressive and Creative Arts – (English, Drama, Music, Art)
2   Science and Technology (Including HE)
3   Languages and Humanities
4   Maths (supported by PE staff for pastoral work to make up necessary numbers)
5   A cross-curricular team led by the Senior Teacher responsible for PE and Community Sport
6   Learning Support – Special Needs, Computer Assisted Learning, Library, Careers, Resources, Multi-cultural monitoring and emphasis.
The teachers of five of the groups of subjects take responsibility for

tutoring one Year of the school. Teams 1–4 work on a rotating basis with Years 2–5, while Team 5 stays permanently with the 11+ entry and liaises with primary schools. Because Team 5 has members from most subjects they are responsible not just for the pastoral care of the intake year group but teach the majority of their timetable. The extra team, Team 6, is not a separate group of people but is made up of members of staff from the other teams. They have no separate tutorial responsibility but support the curriculum work, academic and pastoral, of the other teams.

In each of the teams formed by grouping the subjects there is a specialist in pastoral work – usually one of the previous Heads of Year on a 'B' allowance – whose function is the support of the tutoring role of the members of the team. Although the title Head of Year for that B post has been retained, for a variety of internal reasons, the overall management of both the curriculum area and the pastoral function is in the hands of the Team Leader of each group. Each of the groups therefore contains a number of Standard Scale teachers and a number of B/C allowance teachers, one of whom is the pastoral specialist.

For example, Team 4 – Science and Technology – is structured like this:

Team Leader (E)

| Head of Science (B) | Head of Year (B) | Head of Technology (B) |

Six Main Scale or A allowance teachers

The Team Leader and the Head of Year usually have no tutorial responsibility, but the two heads of subject and the six main scale teachers can each have a form in any one year. Promotion to the position of Team Leader can be from either a subject or a pastoral base, since the task of the Team Leader is to manage both. The six Team Leaders, with the Head and two Deputies, form the Senior Management Team of the School. The position of the pastoral 'Head of Year' becomes much more of an advisory post and, as in the Valley School, 'first among equals' with a specialist function.

PSE is delivered partly through the tutor teams and partly through support teams, which consist of all of the 'non-tutors' amongst the staff including the Head and Deputies. The availability of the support teams makes it possible for the tutors to use some PSE time (which is timetabled simultaneously across the school in six-week blocks) for individual withdrawal of pupils for review and guidance.

For a variety of reasons – in reponse both to pressures created by other changes and to discontent with what existed – Highlands School and Valley School have moved towards a pastoral model which recognises the increased importance of tutoring, creates teams of teachers who share both academic and pastoral responsibilities, and emphasises the supportive and advisory role of the pastoral specialist. Neither school has moved as far in this direction as the Biddick School (*TES* 4th April 1986 p18) or the Knowle High School in Blackpool (*TES* 3rd February 1989 pA26) in which the tutor is the 'linchpin' of the schools' work, and in which the pastoral/academic split seems to have disappeared ('pastoral' is a word they no longer use at the Biddick School); but both have moved in a similar direction. The pressures which created that movement are not specific to Highlands and Valley Schools but exist in all schools in our sample.

The first of these pressures for change is an increasing awareness of the disadvantages of the Head of Year or House structures created in the early 1970s. Both schools have recognised, for example, that those structures helped to create, or at least contributed to, a pastoral/academic division which they felt to be harmful and limiting to both teachers and pupils. This, of course, is a view now increasingly shared. Keith Kirby, in the SCDC/NAPCE publication *Whole Person: whole school* (1989), notes that 'The traditional pastoral structure' had been rejected by each of the three schools he studied, as they 'sought to unify the teacher's disparate functions' and HMI have recently expressed concern about the lack of integration and the existence of underlying tensions between pastoral and academic systems (HMI 1989). Bloomer's conclusion that the system of pastoral care in the school that he investigated 'created and aggravated pastoral problems it was designed to help' and Tattum's comments on the 'bureaucratization' of pastoral care illustrate further discontents.

The 'traditional pastoral structures' have, unfortunately, fostered the idea that pastoral work is best left to specialists; hence the pastoral role and responsibility has been taken away from the teacher and form tutor, in spite of the rhetoric of staff handbooks and job descriptions of form tutors. The 'referral upwards' pattern so common in pastoral hierarchies has meant that pastoral Heads have been snowed under dealing with crisis situations and re-active work, largely about discipline. Too rarely have they had the chance to be pro-active and to work positively to support tutors since the system, in which they have both been entrapped, has made it necessary for tutors to pass things on; there has developed, inevitably, an element of 'S/he's paid to do it'. As a telling illustration of this a year Head recently complained to us that a member of staff had stopped him in the corridor and said 'Your lot are throwing paper around in the playground over there.'

Inevitably too, in the 'referral upwards' pattern, the status of the tutor suffers, as both Douglas Hamblin and Delwyn Tattum have pointed out, since in the eyes of the pupils they are seen to lack power. This lack of institutional power is translated by the pupils into a lack of personal power as an individual or as a personal weakness. As one pupil said recently 'The trouble with the teachers in this school is they can't stand up for themselves.' It is also seen by many staff as a vote of no confidence in them by the senior management. 'I know Denise and her mother very well,' said one tutor, 'and Denise has asked me to go down and talk to them both. But I'm not allowed to do that.'

The Elton Report (1989), while focusing more narrowly on discipline in schools, strongly reinforced many of these discontents with present systems. They found, for example, (p92) that 'schools which achieve good standards tend to deal with disciplinary problems where they happen and at the lowest level' and they note that referral upwards of problems 'reduces the authority of the class teacher and gives status to misbehaviour'.

> 'Such systems also tend to become overloaded because senior staff are dealing with an endless stream of minor offenders.'

The Elton Report recommended (R37, p112):

> 'that secondary headteachers and teachers should base pastoral systems on the strengths of the traditional, integrated academic, welfare and disciplinary role of the teacher.'

Here again the Elton Report was reflecting an increasing discontent with the way in which pastoral structures have fostered the pastoral/academic divide. In both the schools we have described, the need was seen to re-structure their pastoral systems in ways which underlined and reinforced the dual – or as Elton suggests, triple – role of all teachers. In the Highlands model for example, the D/E Team Leaders have responsibility for discipline within the Year, as well as within the subjects, supported by the Head of Year and Heads of subjects. Discipline is seen as a management task, fundamental to a whole-school and whole-pupil approach, not something the 'pastoral side' takes care of in order to allow the 'academic side' to proceed. The close and often ignored connection between disruption in the classroom and poor teaching and inappropriate content has always made such a division a nonsense anyway.

Another major disadvantage of the traditional structures, from the teachers' point of view, is that of having to specialise, at a relatively early stage in a career, in either pastoral or subject teaching work and to look for promotion from then on within one or the other of the two hierarchies. At a time when Heads of Year or House could be on Scale 3 or Scale 4, and a Head of upper/lower school on Scale 4 or senior teacher, progression to pastoral deputy was possible. Developments over the past few years, however, have made this progression less likely.

In the first place deputies are adopting more general management roles, following the implementation of the 1987 School Teacher's Pay and Conditions of Employment Order, under which the deputy inherited to a greater degree the overall responsibility of the Head. Within many senior management teams, while there is still a degree of specialisation and area responsibility, tasks are being shared and are seen as joint responsibilities, while each deputy is able to stand more clearly 'in the place of' the Head at any time. At least at that level the movement is towards corporate or collegiate responsibility and functioning.

Parallel to that movement, the salary structure created by the 1987 settlement changed the status of the old Scale 3 post. Prior to 1987 it was seen clearly as a middle management position, with two grades beneath it, and at first only one, later two, grades above it. From 1987 however, since 'A' posts can be given temporarily, and for merit or for a specific and limited task, the B allowance to which the old Scale 3 posts transferred has become the first permanent promoted position above the Standard Scale, with now not two, but three grades between that and the deputy Head level. Since the majority of pastoral posts were held on a Scale 3, now a B allowance, movement from there to a deputy Headship is far more difficult, and early specialism in a separate pastoral care function could be a career dead-end.

The management reorganisation at Highlands School is aimed precisely at that difficulty. D and E allowance positions are seen as overall management posts, neither pastoral nor academic but both, and promotion to them – from within the school or without – can be from either a pastoral or an academic background. This opens up clear channels of opportunity and training in management to both pastoral and academic staff. It becomes possible, and has recently happened, to transfer from Head of Year to Head of subject, on the same Scale and within the same team. The two parallel hierarchies described in the earlier literature on pastoral care or school management cease to exist; pastoral expertise becomes much less of a special and separate territory and much more a supportive function for tutorial work. The expertise still exists and is still developed, but it is seen in this model as adding to a teacher's competence and chances of promotion, not limiting them permanently to pastoral work and eroding their credibility as subject teachers, possible Heads of Department or future overall managers.

While the Valley School has not, to the same degree, changed its management structures, the same thinking is evident in their appointment of Pastoral Advisers. They are not seen as constituting a separate division of the school; the appointment is either an additional responsibility for someone already on a B/C/D allowance, which they accept for a time because of interest and/or experience, or it is given, again for a time and with an A allowance, to someone on the Standard Scale to add to their strengths and depth of experience. The time period of course is not necessarily limited, and is measured in years rather than months, but the specialism and development of expertise do not mean a permanent movement into a separate career channel.

The greatest pressure for change in pastoral systems has been the remarkable increase in one-to-one work demanded by, for example, TVEI, RBA, Profiling, GCSE Course Supervision, Review and Guidance and Active Learning – to name but six. Each of these innovations has both pastoral and academic aims and uses what might be described as pastoral skills to achieve academic ends. Since each pupil has to be 'guided' individually or in a very small group, on a structured and regular basis, sheer logistics demand that almost all staff have to be involved, and most schools are using the tutorial system as the obvious structure by which they can ensure the work is done. Tutoring might be said to be coming into its own. Schools have for years described the building of a positive relationship with the pupils of a form as a responsibility of the form tutor, but as Tattum pointed out, when anything important happened the pastoral Head was supposed to take over, so that the potential of the relationship was wasted. Now however, with the growth of one-to-one work, that positive relationship can and should be used to help the school achieve its academic aims. In fact such a relationship – one of confidence and trust with the 'significance' described in Chapter 5 – is fundamental to the success of 'profiling' or any other of the innovations described above. The task of tutoring has increased enormously, both in difficulty and in importance, and for the first time is seen to have a clear function in the central academic process of the school.

This is why some schools in our sample have increased the number of form tutors so that in Years 10 and 11, for example, form size can be just 12–16 pupils. Others are both increasing the numbers of tutors and emphasising the importance of tutoring by using senior management as form tutors. Another solution, with an interesting split in functions, has been to make every 'spare' teacher in the school – including the Head – responsible for tutoring, although not register marking, a small group of 5 or 6 pupils in Years 10 and 11.

The importance of the tutoring activity clearly has been reinforced by the new, and very specific, contractual obligations under which all teachers are now expected to be:

> 'Promoting the general progress and well-being of individual pupils and of any class or group of pupils assigned to him,' *and* 'Providing guidance and advice to pupils on educational and social matters.'
> *(School Teacher's Pay and Conditions of Employment Document 1987)*

For the first time this has been written in black and white. Our impression however, is that while the reinforcement can be seen as useful and timely no school has yet changed its pastoral structure because of the pastoral responsibilities written into the new contracts, and that so far at least they have had little impact on any tutor's perception of their tutorial function. Perhaps for this to happen we need a generation of teachers removed from the strife of the past few years, and accepting the contractual obligations from the start as a part of their teacher role.

Two relatively minor administrative benefits were seen by Highlands School and Valley School to come from their re-organisation of their pastoral structures. The first is that putting together subjects as the basis for one year's tutoring solves the geographical problem of having the pupils in one Year spread throughout the school building, since subjects occupy distinct areas of the school. Secondly, under the pressure of '1265 hours', the scheduling of meetings has become difficult in many schools – perhaps just once a month for a pastoral team. The new structure in Highlands School enables the same group of teachers to meet more frequently and allows them to decide their own priorities (pastoral, academic or both) for any given meeting.

The task of tutoring in the two schools has been seen to have grown, to have become more explicit, more central and more important, and in terms of the work done by the tutors has meant a move from tutor 'subordination' towards tutor 'ascendancy'. Neither school has thought or talked in those terms however. Marland's original descriptions hint at a power struggle over 'territory'; the power to write letters to parents for example, or the power to be involved in decisions. The 'new' tutor may have both of these powers but this has not meant, in a see-saw fashion, a consequent diminution in the power of the pastoral Head. In a sense, the battle over 'territory' has become irrelevant since the 'territory' has both expanded and moved. The new tutoring work is not just different in degree from what went on before, but different in kind; because it involves every pupil it is not something that can be undertaken by the pastoral Head. The tutors have additional and different work to do, which demands as its foundation the relationship it has always been the tutors' task to develop, a relationship which can never be matched for all pupils by the one pastoral specialist in each Year. Strengthening and using the tutor/pupil relationship may make the tutors more obviously the persons to deal with other pastoral tasks, and they may in that sense become more 'ascendant'; but they are also, in the two schools described, now more directly accountable to the pastoral Head or Team Leader for the quantity and quality of tutoring delivered. This is made possible because the increase in 'Review and Guidance' work means that tutoring becomes a more overt and explicit activity, with outcomes (particularly in the form of personal target setting) which affect, and can be seen by, all subject teachers. It also reflects the revolution in the whole concept of teacher management, emphasised and given impetus, but not created, by the 'Conditions of Service' imposed on teachers in 1987. With more direct accountability, and particularly with the introduction of appraisal, there is far less chance of those idiosyncratic definitions of the tutors' job that have bedevilled pastoral work, and even less chance that tutors and managers can define it as differently from each other as those we described in Chapter 4.

Tutors and their managers – and also their managers, the senior management – together constitute a system, the essence of which is that one part cannot change without the other parts also changing. As the process of tutoring develops and changes there must be a corresponding change in emphasis in the work of the pastoral specialists, the Heads of Year, senior tutors or pastoral advisers. This will not happen easily, nor instantly; the habits and attitudes of 'referral upwards', and of the pastoral Head taking over responsibility, have developed deep roots over the past twenty years, and for most teachers are an accepted norm of school life. Changing the title will certainly not be enough.

The pastoral specialists – Advisers or Year Heads – will have to extend their roles and develop new skills. They will have to devise ways of encouraging form tutors to accept a fuller pastoral responsibility – including those who in the past may have wished to do more and those also who may have embraced the constraints of the system willingly. Instead of doing the job themselves they will have to develop the skills necessary for the supervision, support, guidance and training – essentially the management – of form tutors, for which their earlier experience may not have equipped them. As the pastoral deputies pointed out (Chapter 4), 'Good ones (tutors) have got on with the job. Bad ones have been compensated for by Year Heads'. It will no longer be enough merely to compensate for another's apathy or errors. The job of the Year Head, or pastoral adviser, will not be to take over problems or difficult children in order to deal with them more effectively than the tutor could, but to manage and lead a team of tutors. In the words of the Valley School's definition the pastoral adviser's role is:

'To enable and facilitate the work of the form tutor who is primarily responsible for the students in her/his own tutor group.'

For many pastoral specialists this is not a different role of course, and will merely mean a change of balance and emphasis between the new job and the old. Others, however, will in their turn need much supervision, support and guidance – and training – from senior management, when letting go their previous styles of working and adopting new ones. This means that there must be a whole-school awareness of the changes that are taking place, and whole-school policies to support those changes. It must be recognised that if the job of the tutor changes the job of the pastoral specialist changes, and that therefore the job of the senior management with the pastoral specialists changes also.

Put simply, if tutors are expected to take on a fuller role with major responsibility for their charges then the tutors have a right to expect support and help in the work that fuller role demands – not to have someone take over when it becomes difficult or important, but to have support in taking the responsibility. In the words of the Elton Report

'The primary aim of management support should be to increase teachers' capability to solve their own problems.'

The tutor will need not only support from management, middle and senior, but support from colleagues, support from procedures and support from the school ethos, the basic assumptions and attitudes dominant in the school. This in its turn will mean developing a relationship of trust between the tutors and their managers, a trust – in the tutor's professional competence – implicitly and significantly absent in the previous 'referral upwards' processes.

We can illustrate such a relationship working in practice by going back to John Rivers and examining how he and his managers deal with some of the situations which were noted in his Log Book at the beginning of Chapter 5.

9
New Relationships

'I believe that most schools have a massive ability that is being underused because heads don't trust their staff.'

(Head of Biddick School, TES 4th April 1986)

Peter Wilson

Peter Wilson, you may remember, had been thrown out of the History room before the lesson started, for entering the room shouting. He had spent the lesson under supervision in the 'Time Out' room which usually leads to 'going on report'. Mrs Young, the History teacher, had written a note about this to John and had reinforced that note by comments in the staffroom at breaktime. Peter, and others who were in the same lesson, state that on this occasion Peter had said and done nothing, but that others had been making the noise and that Mrs Young's back had been turned. Mrs Young expects Peter to be punished and for his behaviour to change, and expects John to work on this.

John's first action is to sit down and talk with Peter. Whatever the rights and wrongs of this incident the relationship between Peter and Mrs Young has obviously gone wrong over a period of time. Peter admits that there have been a number of occasions when he has been awkward, that he and Mrs Young have had rows before and that she expects him to cause trouble. John describes the process to Peter as 'tying a label round his neck' and asks him to think up ways of getting rid of the label.

John's second action is to discuss the matter with his Year Head, alerting her to the problem and stating his intention to talk to Mrs Young. In fact Mrs Young had already been to the Year Head to register her annoyance with Peter, so she already had one view of the problem. However, as John sees it there are a number of conflicting and confusing aspects to it:

a There is a long–term difficulty between Peter and Mrs Young which needs dealing with.

b Similar instances have occurred between Mrs Young and a number of other pupils.

c Peter's behaviour in other lessons is by no means perfect, but not a major concern.

d Peter is possibly innocent of provocative action on this occasion.

e To follow standard procedures and put Peter on report for an incident in which he may be innocent is likely to increase his sense of injustice, of being 'picked on', and alienate him further both from Mrs Young and from the school.

What emerges from the discussion with the Year Head is that John will explore with Mrs Young the long–term problem with Peter. He will hope for an acceptance on her part that on this occasion she may have been wrong to throw Peter out, but even if this is not possible he wants an agreement with her that action is not taken on this incident in view of the primary importance of the long–term work. If the crisis can be removed, then long–term work becomes more possible.

John's third action then, is to talk with Mrs Young, and his fourth is to go back to Peter to look at strategies for removing the label. What he is working towards is an effort on Peter's part to change and an awareness of that effort by Mrs Young. When the two movements are taking place side by side they will reinforce each other.

The role of the Year Head here is not to take over the problem, talk to Mrs Young herself or interview Peter, but to support, help and enable John to take those steps himself. The degree of support, suggestion and help needed will of course depend on the skills and experience of the tutor, and for John little more is needed than the agreement of a mutual strategy. But it is important for John, as for any tutor, that he feels he is not working in isolation, that the strategy is mutually agreed, and that he is working in harmony with his immediate supervisor.

Jason Dodds

The same criteria apply to John's second situation, that of Jason Dodds' mother and her anger over the visit of the Education Welfare Officer. John has suggested that he and Mrs Dodds meet to talk over the problem, and he has left the initiative for that meeting with her. But if his message is not passed on, or is ignored, John feels he must try again to meet her. Jason's attendance has been very irregular, and the visit of the EWO was timely and necessary. This may have an effect on Jason's attendance, and the

EWO may continue to work with the family, but John is concerned about the mother's anger with the school and feels that it can only be harmful to Jason's work, attitude and behaviour.

His first action is to talk with the EWO about the visit and about any further work the EWO is likely to do with Mrs Dodds and Jason. His second action is to mention Jason's case to his Year Head. Again he is not looking for permission to take action or necessarily looking for advice on how to proceed. He is alerting the Year Head to the problem with Jason and to his own proposed action, and is able to proceed with that action mutually agreed. When Mrs Dodds fails to respond to his message, he writes making an appointment for him to visit after school.

Our third illustration of the tutor/management relationship is John's reception of Marie Richards into his form.

Marie Richards

Admission procedures in John's school, for children transferring from other secondary schools, follow a standard pattern. When the parents approach the school they and the prospective pupil are seen by the Head or a Deputy. Provisional agreement is usually made then that the pupil is to be admitted and information about the school – prospectus, uniform lists and, for the upper school, option sheets – are given to the parents. The Year Head is informed, introduced to the parents if possible, and then has the task of making enquiries to the previous school. An appointment is made for the form tutor, sometimes the form tutor and the Year Head, to see the parents and their child – such as John's Thursday appointment with Marie and her parents. That meeting is to 'get to know each other' and the tutor explores the new pupil's feelings about moving and attitudes to the previous school. Decisions are made about options, timetables and homework requirements are discussed and arrangements are made to receive the pupil. One of the members of the same form is usually introduced who will 'befriend' the new girl or boy in the first few days.

Marie and her parents had been seen by the deputy Head earlier in the week. They had just moved into the area, following the father's change of job, and had approached the school since it was their nearest one. Both Marie and her parents expressed themselves as pleased with what they had seen and heard of the school, and seemed anxious for Marie to do well. There was space in the year group and no reason why they should not admit Marie, but some of their replies to the deputy Head's questions about Marie's previous work seemed rather evasive, and although admission was agreed there was an obvious need for further information.

Before John's interview with Marie and her parents therefore, the Year

Head had been in contact with Marie's previous school, had asked for records to be sent on and had also had a discussion about Marie with her Head of Year in that school. What she had heard was rather disturbing. Marie had had a lot of absence over the past year, much of it unexplained, and seemed to have caused a considerable degree of disturbance when she was in school – frequent disagreements with other pupils, not very much work done, violent arguments with members of staff, and disappearance from school following the arguments. She had been excluded from school for short periods on two occasions for using abusive language to staff and the school had been considering a longer term, or possibly permanent, exclusion when she left, since the shorter periods had done little to change her behaviour.

John, therefore, has a potentially difficult interview on Thursday morning. After the contact with Marie's previous school he, the Year Head and the Deputy spend some time discussing how to handle the interview and what strategies they can use to prevent the same pattern starting again.

They decide that both John and the Year Head will be present at the meeting with the parents. The Year Head will report to the parents the conversation she has had with Marie's previous school, will emphasise that they must try to prevent the previous pattern of absence and misbehaviour from being repeated, and that this will mean close co-operation and communication between the school and Mr and Mrs Richards. Since John will be the person responsible for implementing the strategies and communicating with the parents, he will outline their proposals, which will also be typed out so that the parents can take a copy away with them.

John's discussion with the parents emphasises the need for regular communication – which will make demands on the parents as well as the school. He will monitor closely Marie's work and behaviour and he proposes to ring them up at the end of each week with a report on this – good or bad. They arrange a time for this phone call to take place. He asks the parents to notify the school immediately – before 9.15 – if Marie is unable to attend, and promises that someone from the school will ring up the parents if Marie is absent without that phone call, or disappears later. He suggests a meeting one month from now in which Marie's progress, and these arrangements, can be reviewed. He also arranges a time in Marie's first week when they can talk for a few minutes about how things are going for her – and he will, of course, see her at registration times. There is some discussion of what the parents can do after receiving the weekly report to apply appropriate rewards or sanctions. The emphasis throughout is on the school and the parents working closely together, and the ultimate responsibility of the parents for Marie's behaviour and attendance. Finally, John introduces Debbie Parsons to Marie and arranges for them to meet in the school foyer on Monday morning.

In this example John is at the centre of decision making and of action. Both the Deputy and the Year Head have been involved and taken some of the work and responsibility. John has the central part to play, but he does so having been involved in creating the strategy and with the knowledge of full support from his management.

With these three specific examples of tutor work in mind, and against the background of the questionnaires reported in Chapter 4, we checked with our sample schools on the part the tutor and Year Head would normally play in dealing with them.

In most of the schools Peter would be referred to the Year Head as a discipline problem and the Year Head would do the talking to Mrs Young.

In some of the schools the tutor would make contact with Mrs Dodds, the angry mother, but in most of them, where there was likely to be a difficulty with a parent, the Year Head or Deputy would take the interview.

In most of the schools the tutor would be told that a new pupil was arriving but would play no part in the induction and would be very unlikely to interview the parents. The Deputy was equally or more likely than the Year Head to make contact with the previous school, and be involved in the follow-up process when there were obvious problems.

The normal pattern then, as we suggested in Chapter 4, seems to be that when any problem goes further than the form tutor talking to a pupil as an initial disciplinary action, when negotiation with other members of staff or contact with parents is needed, when tact, firmness, diplomacy or authority is required, schools cease to trust the form tutors; the situation is taken out of their hands and action is taken further up the hierarchy. As Delwyn Tattum points out (Tattum 1982), only when something is seen as 'insignificant' is it left in the tutor's hands.

What this method of dealing with difficulties does, as we have previously noted, is downgrade the status of the tutor and confirm the pastoral/academic divide. It creates an 'us and them' relationship between the pastoral hierarchy – those who can be trusted, in Eric Lord's words, to 'mediate between the school and the community' and those, the 'ordinary' teachers and tutors, who cannot; more importantly it leaves untapped and unused the potential and expertise of tutors most of whom, as we showed in Chapter 3, are experienced teachers and managers in other areas of the school. As the Head of Biddick School said, in the words we used at the beginning of this chapter:

> 'We achieve what we achieve by trusting teachers. I believe that most schools have a massive ability that is being underused because heads don't trust their staff.'

In John's school the trust the management have in the competence of the tutor is emphasised and is at the root of all working relationships. On the basis of that trust power of action and decision has been moved down the hierarchy and management assumes its proper function of supporting, enabling, monitoring and supervising – and concentrating on the decisions and action proper to its role. The management also increases its contact with larger numbers of pupils rather than having to concentrate on the miscreant few.

The rationale for taking the work out of the hands of tutors, as has happened over the last twenty years, seems to be based on three clusters of arguments.

The first of these can be summed up as 'the job of teachers is to teach'. Of course it is! But implicit in this line of argument is the idea that the job of the pastoral structure is to take care of the problems, behavioural and emotional, angry parent or awkward colleague so that 'teaching' can proceed undisturbed. Implicit also is the idea that behaviour displayed in the context of the classroom can be 'cured' outside the classroom and that the pupil, purged of emotional difficulty and more amenable, can then be returned. In this model teaching is apparently an exercise in pure pedagogy, performed with a group of 'biddable adolescents' which is, to say the least, unreal. It is also probably unproductive and self defeating. As Robert Laslett commented (Laslett 1985)

> 'Managing it (disruption) certainly takes away from instruction time, but whether it wastes teacher's time is less evident. If working with biddable adolescents is all there is to teaching, then this suggests that there is no value to teachers and pupils in difficult interchanges between them, awkward as these may be.'

As far as the form tutor is concerned it is the evidenced involvement and concern of the 'ordinary' teacher with the problems, feelings and behaviour of their pupils – with the reality of their lives – which will enable the classroom to be an place of growth.

The second cluster of arguments suggests that the ordinary form tutor lacks the authority to speak for the school, and that parents prefer to speak to someone in authority.

The second part of that argument may be true, but whether the form tutor can speak for the school, or is seen to have authority, depends totally on the policies and structures of the school and the image given out of the status of tutors. If the tutor is trusted as a competent professional and is involved in the decision making process then the tutor has the status and authority to 'mediate with the community', to deal with angry parents and with colleagues. The third cluster of arguments for 'referral upwards' suggests that tutors are so busy teaching that they haven't time to deal with problems. Of course there is some truth behind this and both Year Heads and Deputies also suffer acutely from lack of time. A more generous staffing ratio which reflected the reality of the job would help enormously – but this seems unlikely to be achieved in the majority of schools within the staffing constraints of the early 1990s. In some schools, however, tutors do deal with things which in other schools are handled only further up the hierarchy, and to some degree at least it becomes again a matter of school priorities. As an example, if someone in the school has to deal with twenty problems outside the classroom, per day, each of which takes about thirty minutes, the school can give two people five hours each or twenty people thirty minutes each. Of course this is simplistic arithmetic, but how a school allocates its 'dealing with difficulties time' is a matter of school policy, and some schools do find ways to create at least some contribution to the time that a tutor would need.

The arguments seem to us a rationale based on the thinking, structures and practices of the last twenty years which are now being reviewed and re-thought. What we are suggesting, and what is illustrated by John Rivers' work with the three situations described above, is an inversion of those practices. The key factor in dealing with each situation is John's relationship with, and responsibility for, his form; each step in the process both uses and strengthens his relationships with the individuals in that form. The Year Head's job is not to take over the work but to accept John's primary position and to advise, guide, support and supervise John's efforts. In this model the Year Head's experience and expertise are recognised and used but so too is John's competence; he is not de-valued and de-skilled by having anything 'significant' or difficult taken away. In a similar fashion the role of the deputy Head is to support and supervise the work of the Year Head. The form tutor stays at the centre and the work of 'management' is to support the task of tutoring.

We noted earlier that for tutors to take on the fuller role we have described above they needed support, not only from management but from 'the school ethos, the basic assumptions and attitudes dominant in the school'. One example of this is the degree to which the school ethos expects or permits tutors to represent their pupils, or to speak for them when there are difficulties with the system or with other members of staff; in effect, to use Tattum's word, to act as '*advocate*' for them.

> '*The tutor as advocate* would have the authority to intervene on a pupil's behalf and would so truly represent his best interests *vis-a-vis* other teachers.... The pupil would then have someone to speak for him, represent his best interests, in a system which confronts him with a whole range of problems.'
> (*Tattum 1984*)

This concept has been translated into action in some schools. The article on Knowle Hill School in the *TES* describes a tutor as 'the pupil's mentor, agent and protector of her interests against the system,' while the Valley School's description of the 'Role of the Form Tutor' states that

> 'The form tutor is the student's personal tutor over a period of five years. This will mean that the form tutor will act as advocate for the student in all matters relating to school so that the student always has someone to speak for them in any situation which may arise.'

We suggest that it is the school or staffroom ethos that gives permission for the advocate role to be adopted because, while it can be written into expectations and job descriptions, the degree to which it can work in practice will depend on its level of acceptance by the staff as a whole. There will be, for example, an obvious conflict at times between that role and the very strong staffroom ethos of group loyalty. Nevertheless, the advocate role is a natural corollary to John Rivers' position of primary responsibility for his form, where the conditions that Tattum suggests are necessary for it already exist.

> 'It would require a redistribution of authority so that tutors have greater
> powers of discretion, greater personal autonomy and a direct involvement
> in decision-making procedures. They would adopt a more purposive role,
> interviewing parents, contacting outside agencies, and even challenging
> the system at any level if they are convinced that a pupil has a genuine
> grievance.'   *(Tattum 1984)*

We have already seen one example of John as advocate for a pupil in his form in his dealing with Mrs Young over Peter Wilson. A similar example is given in the Knowle Hill article where the Head cites

> 'the case of a pupil who, at a review with his tutor, confided that although
> he had countersigned it, a profile in one subject stating that homework
> was rarely completed, wasn't fair because the teacher never set home-
> work. The tutor was obliged to take the matter up with the teacher on the
> pupil's behalf.'

A further illustration of John's advocacy role, which also raises the question of staff group loyalty, is his work with the whole form over their difficulty in the English lesson.

The English lesson

Once again, as with Peter and Mrs Young, there is obviously a long-term difficulty between the English teacher, Mr Smithers, and John's form – to which both parties contribute. John's work with his form has emphasised their degree of responsibility for what is going on and their responsibility for trying to put things right. But he is well aware that this is only part of the story. His opinion, based on previous knowledge of his colleague as well as the form's description of the incident, is that Mr Smithers, the English teacher, could and should have handled the situation differently, that he over-reacted and turned what was a minor piece of disruptive behaviour into a major confrontation with the whole class. Mr Smithers must, therefore, bear some of the responsibility for the outcome. From John's own point of view this is annoying, since he feels he is having to pick up the pieces from a colleague's mistakes. More importantly however, he is faced with a professional and ethical dilemma. His loyalty to 'his' form, his sense of justice, as well as the probable consequences of being unfair to them, make it impossible for him to pretend even to them that they alone are to blame. But, as we mentioned earlier, his loyalty to a colleague, and more strongly to the staff group of which he is a member, prevents him from talking openly with the form about Mr Smithers' behaviour or asking them questions about it. Inevitably his loyalty to his staff group (if not to Mr Smithers), his concept of how far he can go in talking about a colleague to pupils, inhibits honest and open discussion with the form about what really happened. As a Headteacher writing in the *TES* about the tutor's role said, 'Loyalty and honesty, for example, prove to be uneasy bedfellows in the classroom' (Roger Harris 1987).

This is not a new problem of course – all staff, particularly those with senior pastoral responsibility, face this difficulty daily. Some we have discussed this problem with accept that individuals or small groups of children can, in the privacy of an office, discuss frankly their feelings about other members of staff. Others, like one deputy Head we spoke to, walk a different tightrope:

> 'Well, I do encourage the children to come and talk to me – I like to make it clear that they can come to talk about anything that is worrying them. Not about people of course – about members of staff. I think that would be very wrong. They can talk about the subject, but not about the teacher.'

It can be argued that in a school where, to quote the 'Aims and Goals' document of Valley School, 'The primary purpose of the school is to benefit each of its students', John's loyalty to his form should take priority over his loyalty to a member of staff. On the other hand it will benefit none of the students if the staff are in a permanent state of dissension and feel unsupported by each other. Whatever they would say in private to individuals or small groups of pupils, no-one we consulted would disagree with John's decision not to discuss openly with his form his opinion of Mr Smithers, since this may well leave the form feeling unsure about the boundaries to their own behaviour and will certainly increase Mr Smither's difficulties.

John must however, in his role as 'advocate', make it clear to his Year Head that he does not accept his form's total responsibility for the conflict. He must also discuss with Mr Smithers what he intends to do with the form and make him aware of any efforts to improve things so that Mr Smithers can make a positive response. This discussion in itself, conducted in the right spirit, might be of positive help, but if Mr Smithers insists that the form is punished for their disruption John will have to give the reasons for his reluctance, and ultimately defend himself not only to Mr Smithers but probably before the forum of staffroom opinion. The long-term help and training Mr Smithers needs is a task of management, but John has at least reinforced the management's awareness of a problem area, and must be able to do this without a feeling of disloyalty.

David Beighton

As a final example of the tutor in relationship to colleagues, the management and the institution, let us use John's discussion with David Beighton, a boy in his form.

John's log book contains the item:

> Had a word with David B who has been very quiet since Christmas – sitting on his own and not talking to the others etc. He does not want to talk however – yet – but have made the offer to him – see what happens. Something is wrong somewhere.

When David Beighton did talk to John, some time later, John's feeling that something was wrong was confirmed. Just before Christmas David had been out fairly late one night, playing around in the streets with some friends. The suggestion had been made that they climb over a wall into the yard behind a small off-licence 'just to see if there was anything lying around'. Once over the wall, and in comparative darkness, a window had been forced open and some of the boys had gone in and collected various bottles. They had been disturbed by the police – either checking on the shop or called by an alarm – and all had run away, dropping some of the bottles in flight.

David had climbed over the wall with the others but had not gone into the off-licence, and had not received any of the loot. He had run away when the others did, but had run straight home so had no idea if any of the boys had been identified, and he had since avoided them at school and stayed at home in the evenings. He was aware that the police had been asking questions in the neighbourhood and had been to the school, and he was waiting miserably for them to turn up at his home. His parents, he said, would be shocked and angry at what he had done, since it was the first time he had ever done anything like this, and what they would feel, say and do was what was worrying him most.

John's reaction to this disclosure is to show disapproval of David's behaviour while still making it clear that he is prepared to help. In effect he says 'Look, you've done something stupid and you may have to face the consequences of it. I can't approve of what you have done, but I can see that you're miserable as a result. Let's see what you can do now to clear up the mess, and if I can help.' To repeat the point we made in Chapter 5, John tries to separate out the behaviour from the person and disapprove of the one while supporting the other.

Here, John has to find the balance between his responsibilities to the school, to the pupil, to the parents and to the community. His first principle is to leave David, for as long as possible, with the responsibility to take action to clear up the situation. His second is not to take over from the parents their authority, responsibility and concern. He recognises that the first difficulty is David's worry about his parents' reaction and in discussing this he encourages David to tell his parents about what he has done and offers to support him by going home with him. David rejects this offer but, after rehearsing his confession with John, feels that he can talk with his parents. John suggests that David asks his parents to ring him, and he makes another appointment to see David in a few days' time. In effect he sets a time boundary within which David still maintains control over the situation and has the chance to take action.

This is a key factor in the idea of confidentiality. While someone keeps silent they also, to some degree, keep control, although other processes may of course be taking control out of their hands; the young girl hiding her pregnancy is a good example of this, and police investigation of David's situation is another. However, when someone else is told the secret, power to determine what happens next is handed over. So confidentiality implies a trust, not just 'not to say anything to anyone', but a trust not to take over control, or to take action, or to use the information in a way that might be damaging or painful. This would include making it the subject of staffroom gossip or giving the information to others who might abuse it.

In most counselling work a relationship of trust is created in which the clients can reveal information without having the power of action taken out of their hands, and within which they are encouraged and helped to take action for themselves. There are limits to this of course, particularly for counsellors working with children and young people, and more specifically for teachers receiving information from their pupils, since neither the counsellor nor the teacher is a totally free agent. He or she has responsibilities to employers, to the school, to parents, to the community, to the law and to the care and safety of the pupil which may override any promise given. Had David revealed a situation in which he was being abused at home, for example, and in which he was in any sense 'at risk', John has in law a 'specific duty to care', a duty to take action to ensure David's safety, which is paramount. If John did not take action when he knew David to be 'at risk', regardless of David's wishes, he would be neglecting this duty and would place himself 'at risk' – of prosecution or disciplinary action for this negligence.

John, therefore, carefully avoids making a promise about confidentiality that he may not be able to keep. When David asked him, at the beginning of the discussion, not to tell anyone else, John replied 'I can't promise that

David, because I don't know what you're going to tell me. But I can promise to work out with you what's best to be done, and I can promise not to say or do anything without first discussing it with you.' So although John will not promise total confidentiality he does reassure David that he will not misuse or abuse the information, and that nothing is going to happen behind his back.

Always, promising and keeping total confidentiality is a personal decision for the tutor to make, in which the fact that she or he places themself personally and professionally at risk is only one of the consequences to be considered. We cannot say 'never promise confidentiality' any more than we can say 'confidentiality must always be kept.' What we can point out is the destructiveness of promising confidentiality – by implication or in fact – and then not keeping the promise.

What frequently happens is that the promise is made, or implied or understood, and that the information given is then too threatening to hold. The teacher becomes aware, too late, of the risk they are running or of their own feeling of inadequacy in dealing with the situation. The information is then passed on up the pastoral hierarchy. When the hierarchy is working in a bureaucratic fashion, in a 'referral upward' model, each step in the passing on transfers control from the person passing it on to the person receiving it. It becomes their problem to deal with, their decision to make. Control passes completely out of the hands of the pupil involved, then the tutor, then the Year Head and so on, until finally someone takes action as a matter of policy or principle or to safeguard the school, but without reference to the individuals involved in the chain.

One example of this process was brought to our attention recently when discussing tutorial work with tutors from a number of different schools.

> A girl in Year 9 approached her tutor in some distress and said that she had had intercourse on the previous night with her boyfriend who was in Year 11. This had happened once before and they had vowed that it would not happen again. She now felt very anxious and guilty. She was scared that her mother would find out about it, but also scared of her own lack of control. The tutor discussed both these issues with her, but since she was worried felt it her duty to tell the Year Head, who related this to the Deputy, who told the Head, who interviewed both the girl and the boy and rang up both sets of parents. At no point – from the pupil upwards – was any one person told that the information was being passed on, so the summons to the Head came as a surprise to pupil, tutor and Year Head.

What concerns us here is not the rights and wrongs of what the Head did, but the bureaucratic process whereby control – power to take action – is progressively taken out of the hands of each level of the pastoral hierarchy as the information passes upwards. In fact, in this instance the girl involved short-circuited the process by going home at lunch time and talking with her mother, so that mother's response to the Head's phone call was an undisturbed 'Yes she's told me about it. I said to her last time she should go on the Pill. . . .'

The work of the tutor would seem to have been successful and responsibility for action placed where it belonged – with the girl and her parents. But in the process of upward referral the relationship between the girl and her tutor was damaged and mistrust created between the tutor and Year Head, while the idea that 'serious matters' must be handed over to those above was reinforced. Behind that idea and practice is a lack of trust between one level and the next in both directions and the assumption that, for example, the tutor cannot be relied upon to deal with the matter in an adult and responsible fashion – nor can the Year Head in her turn. The fact that both the tutor and the Year Head feel that they must protect themselves from blame by passing on the problem perpetuates the mythology of inadequacy and demonstrates that, while the senior management do not trust the tutors to deal with the situation responsibly, the tutors in their turn do not trust the senior management to support their actions.

Let us now go back to John Rivers and his problem with David. He is aware that the police have visited the school and spoken with the Deputy about the break-in at the off-licence. He knows that the relationship between the school and the police might suffer if a member of staff is found to have information about the break-in which they have not passed on. He wants, therefore, to report to his Year Head, or the Deputy who spoke to the police, that he has received some information about the break-in, and to discuss with them what he has done about it. But he also wants the matter left in his hands for the next few days and he doesn't yet want to reveal to others the name of the boy involved.

What this demands is a relationship of trust running in both directions. For John to talk openly with his senior management he must feel fairly certain that they will not take over and supercede the arrangement he has made with David: he must trust them to trust him. On their part they must feel that John will deal with the matter responsibly and will not take actions which might damage the school, its relationship with other agencies or with the community. For the management to trust John they need to know what he is doing; indeed for them to support, supervise, monitor and manage John's work there must be open and full communication.

Such communication is vital. Quite deliberately, in John's work with David, we chose a situation which is not particularly threatening in its possible outcomes or dramatic in the way that, for example, child abuse being revealed might have been. When such situations as child abuse are being dealt with, the need for open communication between those involved becomes even more acute. Geoff Myers, a consultant in child abuse procedures with an international reputation and practice, uses the phrase '*We* think better than *I* do' – meaning don't act on your own: consult, communicate, discuss before action – to illustrate the absolute priority that communication has, when critical and highly sensitive matters are being dealt with.

The basis of good communication is the mutual trust we described above. Since John's relationship with his managers is one of trust he can make decisions in the confidence that he will be supported, and he can communicate his actions without fear of being superceded. This does not mean that he cannot be criticised or that suggestions will not be made; but the criticism and suggestions will be to enable him to do the job better, not to take it away from him, and the communication means that he will not be left handling things on his own if they go wrong. As in all the examples we have used of John's work, he keeps the responsibility for the action while management 'supports and supervises'.

We have used John as the 'hero' of this book. He is a 'real' form tutor; we have changed only his name and the school in which he works. We have shown him, we hope, not as 'Superteach' or 'Supertute' but as an ordinary teacher and form tutor with some experience, some understanding of his pupils as well as his subject, a range of skills with small and class-sized groups, and with individuals, and a wish to do an effective job. He is no different in any of these respects from hundreds of secondary school teachers we have met – and no doubt thousands of others.

We have also shown him coping with, and positively – if cautiously – welcoming a wider tutorial function. That wider tutorial role, however, will make demands not only on his professional skills, but on him as a person; it will create pressures on him which he will need support in dealing with and which, as we have emphasised in this chapter, will require appropriate, sometimes new, skills and strategies of management.

In the final chapter we shall use John one more time to examine some of those pressures, on the 'tutor' and on the 'person', and the means by which he can be helped to do a more effective job.

10
Strategies for Support

'... a school is not able to operate one form of care for its pupils and another for staff; to care deeply about one, but neglect the other.'

(Lawley 1985)

Throughout his teaching life, until the last year or so, John Rivers worked within the sort of pastoral system we have described as 'referral upwards', in which problems with and of his pupils, except for minor ones, were 'propelled up the hierarchy' to use Andrea Freeman's words (Freeman 1987): passed on for Year Heads or Deputies to deal with. While the rhetoric of the school's job description for the tutor insisted that he formed 'close and positive relationships' with his pupils, those relationships were neither consistently used nor apparently valued by his managers. Communication with parents – other than reports and Parents' evenings – decisions about pupils, matters of discipline, emotional or behavioural difficulties, all were taken out of his hands. He was expected to 'refer them on' for a solution to be found by expertise elsewhere.

This position made his job both easier and harder; harder, in that as an interested form tutor he was often trying to understand problematic behaviour without the information or knowledge of the background necessary; easier, in that he was not faced with the responsibilities, complexities and contradictions of trying to resolve difficult situations.

When the sort of change came about that we have described in Valley School and Highlands School, with the tutor becoming the centre of the pastoral system, John found that his involvement with the pupils immediately became more complicated although, as he says himself, it also became more satisfying. His job increased in complexity and in responsibility – for listening, for understanding, for working with pupils to find strategies for change, for the whole process of welfare and personal and social development. His advocate role heightened the feeling that he was responsible for 'his' form, a feeling that was reinforced by the fact that the expectations of fellow subject teachers and tutors, for change in a pupil's behaviour for example, were now on him rather than on the Year Head or on senior management.

A consequence of assuming that central responsibility is that John and his fellow tutors have also had to take on board conflicts of role and responsibility that have previously, by and large, been experienced mainly by those further up the pastoral hierarchy. Such conflicts are particularly evident when problems of misbehaviour are being considered; where the demands and needs of the institution often appear to be fundamentally opposed to the needs of the individual. In many a school where the tutor role is not central the Year Head and deputy Head might well have been faced with the following:

> It was agreed at a staff meeting that uniform standards were getting slack, and that all staff, but particularly form tutors, would tighten up on this, warning their pupils and inspecting rigorously each morning for deviations. Anyone not coming up to standard would be sent to the Year Head and on to the deputy if there was no change. The exercise was felt, quite realistically, to be necessary for the image of the school in an area where schools are close together and rolls falling generally.
>
> The tutors, for the most part, did as they were asked with varying degrees of discretion, and a number of pupils filtered through to the Year Heads. For many of these the normal process of demands for full uniform, punishments for not obeying, letters to and discussion with parents and ultimately exclusion, seemed not only futile but unjust. For example, one boy living with an older sister, with intermittent periods 'in care' (since his family had broken up after his father had been sent to prison) had neither the means nor the adults around him to give him the clothes and the structure necessary. Pressure produced some modification of his usual dress but he still regularly turned up at the door of the deputy. The Year Head, well aware of the boy's background, could only gently persuade; other staff, zealously following the agreed line, remonstrated with the boy and commented freely on the lack of 'support' they were getting from 'management'.

When the tutor role becomes central to the school's pastoral system these conflicts move downwards. John and his fellow tutors are now the ones faced with such pressures, and the ones who have to resolve or live with such conflicts.

Explanations and discussions with colleagues and with the pupil, as well as 'welfare work' to provide uniform, can resolve many of tensions in the situation above. More difficult for the tutor would be one where such explanations cannot be given, and where the legitimate expectations of other members of staff, as individuals dealing with a pupil, are at odds with that pupil's needs. For example, in John's school, where the tutor is the prime pastoral agent:

138

A girl in Year 9, whose behaviour had never been angelic, was taken into care after she revealed to her tutor – and afterwards to social workers and the police – that for some years she had been sexually abused by her father. While teachers in the school knew that she had been taken into care, only those immediately involved knew the reasons why, or understood the difficulties she was experiencing in knowing that her father, for whom she still cared, faced a possible prison sentence, that the family had been broken up and that all were experiencing financial hardship because of her revelations. Although her behaviour and language deteriorated sharply following her admission into care, and although her form tutor was inundated with complaints about confrontations and abusive language, there was an obvious reluctance on the part of the tutor and senior staff to apply the normal and visible sanctions. Much time was spent in talking with her, but to staff affronted by her behaviour this seemed weak and inadequate, and the demands for more drastic action increased.

In a situation such as this the 'caring and understanding tutor' sits uneasily with the friend and colleague of those demanding action. The different roles and responsibilities produce obvious and painful conflicts of feeling within the tutor who has to accommodate both.

This conflict between roles, a tension between the needs of the individual and the demands of the organisation or society, is experienced by everyone working with people, young or adult – by teachers or tutors, social workers, counsellors, probation officers, careers officers, medical staff or managers. It is important to realise that the internal conflicts such people experience are an inevitable consequence of doing the job *well*; a direct result of successful empathy with, and understanding of, the people and views on both sides of any question. As Stibbs (1987) noted, the conflicts are normally experienced most acutely by middle management because problems are referred up to them. When the tutor takes on a central role, however, it is no longer possible to pass on those conflicts upwards to management since in a real sense, the tutor becomes the management.

A further change in John's work has been an increased involvement in the pastoral task Eric Lord described as 'mediation and interpretation between school and community' (Lord 1983). This means far more than increased communication with parents; it also means that John has to understand the pupil's and parents' frames of reference and communicate these to the school as well as the school's views to the pupil and parents. He is, as Lord noted, 'in the position of trying to interpret two worlds to each other.' Once again, tasks and problems that, although to some degree involving every teacher, were mainly management responsibilities have been passed down to the tutor level.

When staff are expected to take on the responsibilities of a developed tutorial role therefore, they are exposed to levels of stress and to conflicts of role which deserve and demand support – for the sake of the school and the pupils as well as that of the tutor. Unless support is given such conflicts can create feelings of isolation, can destroy basic trust in colleagues and damage essential working relationships. Unless support is given such conflicts within the individual, between the various roles and responsibilities, are likely to be pushed out as anger and blame on to other members of staff, on to 'senior management' or on to 'the system'. As one member of a pastoral team said, with considerable bitterness,

> 'The trouble is you know, I spend about 90% of my time saying and doing things to kids that I don't want to do but that "the school" or "the staff" expect.'   *(Head of Upper School, 11–16 Comprehensive)*

This is not meant to be taken literally, of course; but it is worrying when one considers the effects of such a feeling on co-operation with colleagues and its possible long-term effect on the individual. As Freeman found, 'continually performing for others' ranked high on a list of stress factors for Year Heads.

In addition to the conflicts of role and responsibilities, working with young people inevitably produces a range of contradictory and ambivalent feelings.

> I want to like them, I try to understand them – I get angry and outraged by their behaviour.

> I want to treat them, and them to treat me, in a friendly way – I want them to obey me when I issue an instruction.

> I want to get close to them, to know them, to understand them. I don't want them to get too close to me; I have a right to areas of privacy.

> I want them to be independent, to speak their minds, to question assumptions – but please not all of the time, only when it's appropriate.

This mixture of feelings is not something new and certainly not confined to those in a pastoral role; it is experienced to some degree by all teachers in any system, tutors or not. But the ambivalence cuts more deeply as the tutor's role is expanded to include direct and prime responsibility for welfare and social development, when the feelings produced can appear to contradict the aims and duties of the role.

When experiencing that ambivalence, or in conflicts of role, tutors can find themselves feeling vulnerable. But understanding and sharing the experiences of the pupils can itself be emotionally demanding. We described above a situation where a young girl revealed to her tutor that she was being abused by her father. The tutor took the necessary steps, the member of staff responsible for dealing with child abuse was informed, social services and the police became involved. Tutors need training in what to do with such information – the necessary processes of recording accurately the gist of what was said, when it was said, and when and to whom the information was passed on. This training is being done in most authorities

140

and expertise in schools is slowly growing. Tutors also need training in how to receive such information, in how to listen helpfully and accurately, and training in this is less common, less available and more time consuming. Even more frequently ignored is the effect of such revelations on the tutor. To listen to such a story is harrowing; it churns the emotions; it hurts. It produces feelings of rage and frustration. 'I wanted to hit something when I heard', said one headteacher, discussing a situation of abuse revealed by one of his pupils. 'I couldn't help thinking about the vulnerability of my own daughter'.

In working with young people, and particularly with their problems and difficulties, tutors use not just professional skills but their own 'self'. Their sensitivities, their values, their feelings are engaged, and indeed are the main tool with which they understand and empathise. Their own personal experiences, good or bad, of being a child and of being a parent for example, are sharply recalled, their personal prejudices are confronted. As we said earlier, it is not just 'the tutor' who needs supporting professionally, but the 'person' – sensitive and vulnerable to stress – behind the role. This seems an obvious point but also one that has been largely ignored in the pastoral literature, and is only recently being addressed by research into teacher stress, for example Dunham (1987).

That personal level of vulnerability is well illustrated, in what Dunham describes as a 'vivid and harrowing manner', by the tutor writing to him prior to a training session.

> 'I would be particularly grateful if the question of coping with bereavement of children in the group could be dealt with – I say this with great feeling, being a tutor in a secondary school where a group is your responsibility for 7 years. In the past 11 years three of my pupils have died and the sisters of two others have also died, and I am at present coming to terms with another pupil who has leukaemia. I am appalled by the insensitivity shown – I have been told of a pupil's death at 9.30am and made an appearance in the classroom to teach at 9.35am! *Any show of grief or shock seems to be taken as a sign of weakness and lack of ability to cope.*'
> *(Dunham 1987) (Our italics)*

In many jobs that are concerned with working with people, and particularly with their problems and difficulties – in social work, counselling, probation work, psychiatry (and increasingly throughout the medical world) and in management and personnel work in industry – support and supervision are seen as essential professional practices. The organisations for which such people work set up systems for offering this, and it is a professional responsibility of the individual worker to use them.

For a variety of reasons this concept has not yet penetrated the educational world to any great extent. The traditional isolation of teachers in 'their territory', the classroom, is perhaps most to blame. At its extreme, the

141

educational ideal seems to be that of independence and self-sufficiency: 'I get on with *my* job in *my* way in *my* classroom'. In schools where that is the ideal, asking for help or admitting difficulties is seen as weakness, as with the tutor quoted by Dunham above, and 'support' is seen as necessary only for those who are failing. As Freeman noted

'The teacher who expresses difficulties and asks for help also runs the risk of being viewed by colleagues as incompetent.'

This is changing of course, but while in many schools it is completely out of date, in many also the mythology of self-sufficiency still lingers. In one school visited by the authors, senior pastoral staff roundly condemned a young colleague who had difficulty in keeping order, largely because their work load was affected, and could only suggest the colleague left teaching. The help offered was to punish the pupils for disruption, which tended to increase their resentment of the young teacher. It was not seen as part of the school's or senior staff's responsibility to offer positive and constructive help which might have prevented the disruption and confrontations.

At a recent conference we heard of a school in which younger female members of staff were to be found crying in the women's cloakroom after school hours; distress and feelings of failure were things that had to be hidden from senior colleagues. At least, although this is small comfort, crying can be a form of release and might lead to a shared relief. The quiet desperation of other members of staff – both male and female – in schools where self-sufficiency is the model, is more damaging both to themselves and to their pupils. Where no overt sign of distress is allowed, where feelings have to be hidden or where the pretence of competence has to be maintained, even shared relief is not possible and the pupils are likely to be on the receiving end, intentionally or not, of the anger behind the teachers' despair.

For schools to develop systems of support for staff, and for staff to participate in them, the damaging myths of the 'self-sufficiency' models need to be thrown away. Asking for help is not an admission of failure. Showing distress at the death of a pupil is not a sign of weakness or of an inability to cope. Acknowledging difficulties is not a confession of incompetence. Support and supervision are not crutches for the less able, the weak and the inadequate. Such concepts form the basis for staff interactions in many schools and contribute hugely to the levels of stress experienced by teachers.

As a basic minimum, schools have a clear responsibility to devise systems and strategies of support and supervision to enable staff to deal with the professional and personal demands the job makes upon them. As HMI noted, one of the key issues in providing effective pastoral care is the need for 'individual tutors to be given sufficient support to perform the role effectively.' (HMI 1989)

Such support is a positive and necessary measure for the professional development, professional security and added competence of all teachers and tutors.

Tutors need, and have a right to expect, support and supervision in a number of aspects of their work. The first of these, although not necessarily in order of priority, is the structural or organisational aspect in which procedures, boundaries of responsibility, relationships with management, other staff and other areas of the school have to be worked out. Stibbs (1987) makes the point that staff care and development

> 'is not just about personal professional satisfaction and growth; it must also be about the inter-relationship among all of the staff and the operation of the whole organisation.'

While clear job descriptions and guidelines can help in this, working relationships, effective procedures and boundaries must be tested in practice and 'fine-tuned' empirically. This is an obvious area for training and the development of skills and responsibility, and support and supervision in this is likely to be offered largely by management.

The second aspect is that of actions and skills with pupils, the development of ideas and strategies; for working with the disruptive pupil for example, or for managing awkward situations. We can describe this as the professional skills or 'craft' level, and support and development in this area can be offered by managers and/or by colleagues.

The third aspect of support, complementing the others, is the personal area of feelings: of inter-personal relationships with colleagues, pupils and parents; of role conflicts; of ambivalence; of emotional response to difficult children, demanding situations and distressing histories. Support at this level is no less a professional need than at the 'craft' level, since the feelings and emotions created will influence, and could well dictate, the actions taken and responses given. Such support may be offered by management, colleagues, or external 'consultants' but it is at least the responsibility of management to make it available.

Freeman approaches the question of support from a different point of view, that of the school's responsibility to 'reduce stressors and improve coping strategies' and suggests that the problem can be analysed at three different levels:

1 *Organisational* – the development of a clear and corporate ethos for caring. Work in the area of management structure and communications to 'ensure a pastoral system able to work'.

2 *Inter-personal* – support systems based on pastoral groups to 'enable individuals to benefit from their colleagues' support and guidance, not only at a morale boosting level but also in the sharing of skills, knowledge and problems.' Recognition that 'stress is not a personal failure but a corporate responsibility.'

3 *Personal* – the development of skills, of better appraisal – specifically self-appraisal – and a problem-solving attitude to difficulties. Basically the development of the skills of stress reduction and management.

(Freeman 1987)

Our own suggestion for a framework of support is based on the need to make tutors more effective, and Freeman's comes from the need to reduce teacher stress; but the areas covered and the suggestions made in each are remarkably similar. Of course, stress and effectiveness are inextricably linked, in that ineffectiveness leads to stress and stress to increased ineffectiveness, and the other way round. It is, perversely, that very link which has meant that the systems of support which would have increased effectiveness have not been more widely introduced. Systems of support have been seen as concerned only with stress reduction and since stress has been perceived as individual weakness, both teachers and schools have been reluctant to adopt those systems.

The climate, however, is clearly changing. Two recent and significant publications, for example, have emphasised the need for teachers to look for – and for management and colleagues to offer – support in their working roles, and have made suggestions which are remarkably similar to each other.

The first of these is the Elton Report which, while concerned basically with increasing effectiveness, points out the inverse relationship between effectiveness and stress, and comments also on what we have called the 'mythology of self-sufficiency'.

> We have described how teachers' traditional reluctance to talk about discipline problems or let their colleagues into their classrooms feeds into a spiral of less effective group management and mounting stress. Support from colleagues as professional equals, which we call 'peer support', is a way of breaking out of that spiral. The peer support group is a valuable resource which is as yet little used in British schools'.
>
> *(Discipline in Schools 1989)*

The report later expands on this to suggest that groups set up to discuss classroom skills must be seen as genuine 'peer support groups', must be voluntary, and are best led by a 'facilitator' coming from outside the school staff, or at least by an experienced teacher 'able to relate well to a wide range of colleagues'. 'The presence of heads and deputies', the report notes, 'could, in some schools, be inhibiting.'

Complementing and reinforcing this, an article on teacher stress in the first edition of *The Teacher* (Vol 1, Spring 1990) makes it clear that schools must 'develop a more co-operative and supportive culture.' The article outlines a plan for 'Colleague Support' suggesting that teachers

- talk things over with their colleagues
- seek advice from more experienced teachers
- take difficult problems to the Head
- obtain reassurance from colleagues that they too feel the same way about the problems they face
- express their feelings to colleagues.

The key idea from these two sources and from others such as Gerda Hanko's book on *Special Needs in Ordinary Classrooms* (Hanko 1985) or the cluster of papers in the NAPCE journal in 1985/7 (Dunham 1987, Freeman 1987, Stibbs 1987, Lawley 1985) as well as from the established practice of other professions, is that talking in a structured way with colleagues, sharing feelings, experiences, ideas and skills, not only reduces stress but increases confidence, professional competence and, for teachers, classroom effectiveness.

The first and major strategy for tutor support is, therefore, the establishment of a procedure by which tutors can talk with colleagues, on a regular basis, about their work. A 'peer support group' is the most obvious mechanism for this, preferably with a non-threatening 'facilitator' who may come from outside the school. Both Freeman and Lawley suggest that a ready-made support group is the tutor team for a House or Year, where meetings already take place and where problems are already shared. This has clear advantages but may also have the disadvantage that the group will have other business in common which may interfere with its support function.

The facilitator's job in such a group is not to advise, train, instruct or even offer expertise, but to convene and chair the meetings and to keep the group 'on task'. Elton suggests that people in an LEA such as Educational Psychologists, Youth Workers and Educational Welfare Officers could well act as facilitators and be a valuable resource, bringing a different perspective to the discussions. Hanko, who is concerned with offering teachers support in dealing with pupils' emotional and behavioural difficulties, develops the idea of a 'consultant', from LEA staff or from specialist staff within the school, to act as an 'informed facilitator – not didactic instructor', in leading the group.

The voluntary support group, with a 'facilitator', is one way for colleagues to share expertise and offer constructive criticism and informed support to each other. A possible alternative is a tutor pairing system based on a 'co-counselling' model, in which a pair of tutors agree to spend time together on a regular basis, taking turns to talk about their own difficulties and successes, and offering help to each other. While this can offer positive support to the individual its development function is more limited. It is easier to set up than group discussions – meeting times can be arranged more easily – but its very informality can be a weakness. Experience suggests that a pair working in isolation from others may, for example, become less rigorous, may more easily develop a habit of task avoidance, and may more easily collude with each other in blaming people outside 'the pair' for any difficulties. Any experienced group leader will be aware that these are common group processes which it is their job to prevent. A pair working without a leader finds it more difficult to avoid these traps.

If tutors, on the one hand, have a need for and a right to support in their work, as we have suggested they do, management, on the other hand, have a duty to supervise and monitor that work. Even where peer support groups or pairs are adopted as the main means of tutor support, some method by which the manager can find out what is happening and exercise some degree of supervision will still be necessary. We have used the words 'support and supervision' in this chapter as if they were two similar and connected activities that belonged together. There is some truth in this, although supervision is more commonly seen as coming from 'above' as a management activity, than from alongside offered by equals. It is a mistake, however, to think in polarised terms of 'support' as uncritical sympathising from a friend and 'supervision' as critical monitoring from above. In their actual practice the two activities can be identical and the words can be used interchangeably. 'Peer support' for example, could well be called 'peer supervision' without altering what happens in the group in the least. Effective support and effective supervision are both processes of listening, understanding and empathising, of friendly but analytic comment and criticism, conducted in an atmosphere of openness and trust.

To a large degree the distinction between support and supervision in practice will depend on the model of pastoral care provision. If pastoral care is 'owned' by the pastoral Head, who delegates certain functions to form tutors, then supervision with an hierarchical emphasis becomes the most likely relationship. On the other hand, if pastoral care is seen as the responsibility of the form tutor, supported and enabled by the pastoral Head, then support and supervision can become identical processes.

A third possible support strategy therefore, is to set up regular supervision sessions for individual tutors by their immediate managers – senior tutors, Year or House Heads. These can provide the necessary support and developmental help for the tutor and also satisfy the management requirements of supervision and monitoring. The fact that there is, at least within the pastoral structure and in the work that is being discussed, an hierarchical relationship between the tutor and manager may create a problem, since it could make it more difficult to establish a relationship of trust. It may be necessary for the manager to start from the basic need to know what is going on, and allow the process to build from sessions which are about sharing information – which is relatively easy – to full support sessions in which feelings and attitudes are shared openly and critical comment is accepted – which is far more difficult.

Support systems, in any case, will not spring suddenly into fully oper-

146

ational and effective being. We referred at the beginning of this chapter to the new skills of management which Year Heads and the like would have to develop, and the skills of supervising and supporting are two of these. Indeed, a significant point for both managers and tutors to understand is that supporting and being supported, supervising and being supervised, are activities demanding skills on both sides, which must be developed by practice and training before they become properly effective.

There is an obvious overlap between the support/supervision sessions just discussed and 'teacher appraisal', not least in the need for the skills to be developed by practice and training. Essentially the skills are the same, and the same questions surround each. Enough has been written on appraisal to make any comment here superfluous, but we do need to point out that teacher appraisal, if properly developed, will act as a further strategy of support, and will enhance the necessary skills.

All schools use 'consultants' from the various support services of the LEA whose work has a direct bearing on that of the form tutor – educational psychologists, educational social workers, counsellors, support teachers for behavioural problems and multicultural specialists for example. The expanded tutorial role requires access to them by the form tutor, and this provides a further level of support and an alternative source of ideas and strategies for working with difficult pupils.

Support and supervision, talking with colleagues, consultants or management about the work and its problems, is becoming increasingly necessary to reduce teacher stress and to improve effectiveness. But there are other practical measures that can be taken to offer support, to spread good practice and make 'being tutored' a more coherent experience for the pupils.

Co-tutoring, for example, could be used far more frequently than it is at present to manage an awkward form, to help a tutor in particular difficulties, or to share a work load. Part-time teachers could be used to go in two or three times a week – with Year 9 at option time, for example. Senior management could be used for this also, for example in the afternoons when they are less likely to be involved in other 'start-of-day' procedures. Teachers without a specific form themselves could be attached to a group of tutors, and have a defined role – maybe to release the tutor to work with small groups or individual pupils. What co-tutoring can do is to offer practical support as well as the chance to talk with someone sharing the task and experiencing the problems at first hand.

Similar to co-tutoring in its advantages is the practice of mutual observation, which can provide a focus for training sessions, making it possible to analyse what happened in particular situations and to examine strengths and weaknesses. The pairing of tutors for mutual support, mentioned earlier, can be tied in with this so that discussion in their support sessions is based on shared knowledge.

As the tutor role changes and increases in complexity, planned induction programmes for teachers joining the staff of a school will become increasingly necessary. This applies not just to probationary teachers but to those, for example, taking up a 'B', 'C' or 'D' post. At the moment such a teacher joining at Christmas or Easter is likely to be thrown in at the deep end of their tutorial work, hopefully to pick up where the previous tutor left off. There is a clear need for a more planned approach to this: perhaps 'shadowing' for a week, or co-tutoring the new form with the Year Head. Previous emphasis on induction for tutoring has been on programmes for probationary or inexperienced teachers – Adams 1986 and Wilcox 1981, for example. These are obviously necessary, but one of the things our own research showed us is that schools differ widely in their expectations of the tutor's functions, and even more widely in their practice; as schools change and move towards new models the differences are likely to increase.

Finally, the place of formal Inset cannot be ignored as a support measure, although training for tutors needs to take place in the context of an overall package of staff development. We mentioned earlier the need for an increased understanding of child abuse procedures, but there are other obvious areas in which school-based training can play a part. Counselling and guidance skills, small group skills, work with parents, an understanding of pupil problems and problem pupils can all be enhanced in this way. Work on disruption – from school procedures and policies down to the sharp end of individual skills and classroom management – is not exclusively a concern of tutors but is a major aspect of their work. Training days in schools can also be used to lay the foundations of support procedures, to develop some of the skills, for example, of supporting and being supported, of supervising and being supervised. What is necessary is that schools recognise tutoring as a central activity involving the majority of staff and allocate it a just proportion of the training time and resources available.

We have suggested above a number of strategies by which teachers' – and specifically tutors' – needs can be met; strategies designed not only to increase effectiveness and encourage professional development, but to relieve feelings of isolation and reduce job-related stress; strategies which create, in effect, a framework for the 'pastoral care of staff'.

The case for establishing such a framework seems to us now to be overwhelming: the increasing evidence of work-related stress and of people leaving the profession; the demands made on teachers by the flux of recent initiatives; by the National Curriculum, the uncertainties of LMS; by widely reported increases in disruptive behaviour; by constant reorganisation; all these make it imperative. Industry has long recognised that a major responsibility of management is the care and development of staff; they are a resource in which a great deal of time and training – and therefore money – has been invested, and it is economic nonsense to neglect them. In education it is even more nonsensical, since staff are the major and most costly resource.

We tend not to think in terms of the 'pastoral care' of staff, restricting the use of that phrase to describe a school's work with children. Lawley (1985) for example, makes the point that while 'care' is seen as appropriate for pupils, teachers are subject to 'management'. But to see these two as opposed or contradictory, as many schools appear to do, is to hold a distorted view both of 'management' and of 'care', and reinforces the 'support is only for the inadequate' view discussed earlier. If a school's idea of 'care' is that of something done or given to pupils by staff – who themselves are too adult to need it – then 'care' ends up, as Lawley points out, reinforcing dominance and emphasising the junior status and inadequacy of the pupils. It becomes patronising and limiting to those on the receiving end, ultimately more concerned with discipline and punishment than with development. Yet, as we have emphasised throughout the book, growth and development – personal, social or academic – is the main purpose of education and specifically of pastoral care.

This same purpose, of growth and development, lies behind the concept of pastoral care of staff. What emerges from our examination of tutor and teacher needs in this chapter, and what schools – staff and management – must recognise, is that 'tutors' needs' and 'pupils' needs' are essentially the same: the fundamental human needs of persons engaged in a task. Staff as well as pupils have a need for 'respectful, accepting and concerned treatment' by 'significant others' – such treatment is the essential core of effective support and supervision. Both staff and pupils have a need for clarity of task and a sense of purpose; a need for boundaries – such as job descriptions or rules – and for space and freedom of action within those boundaries; a need for responsibilities to grow as competence grows; a need to talk about and review their work; a need for support and for friendly and constructive criticism.

Given the similarity of needs it is not surprising that the aims and values, as well as the strategies, behind the support and supervision of tutors bear a close resemblance to those suggested for the tutors' work with pupils. Compare, for example, the process, not the content, of supervision or of appraisal for teachers with that of 'review and guidance' for pupils. Each of these aims at structured and open discussion in an atmosphere of trust, and has a mutually agreed outcome with planned action. Each offers support but recognises and respects the power and responsibility of the individual and each, above all, has development – personal, social, academic or professional – as its main purpose. Because of this similarity of needs and strategies, establishing such systems of staff support has two significant and positive consequences.

The first of these is a practical one. Caring for pupils, in the sense of 'managing their personal and academic development', is an active process which demands skills and expertise. The tutors' experience of being supported develops the necessary skills, offers strategies and provides a model of supportive work which can be applied directly to the care and development of pupils.

Secondly, and perhaps more importantly, the values implicit in staff support create a positive ethos which shapes and influences the ways in which tutors relate to pupils, an ethos of care which is developmental rather than dominating and which is appropriate for adult and young person alike. As Lawley suggests, we need to establish such an ethos, a 'consistent set of values', to run throughout the relationships in a school.

> 'The ethos of staff pastoral care must closely reflect that of the institution's efforts in caring for its children.'   *(Lawley 1985)*

Much as we agree with this, it seems to put the cart before the horse. It is our firm belief that the care of staff, by management and by each other, is not just an end in itself, worthy though that end may be, but the basic and necessary foundation for the school's task of caring for its pupils.

Appendix A

The Real Form Tutor – Statistics

The staffing patterns of 25 schools were examined, with particular reference to the distribution of allowances held by form tutors. The results of that examination, presented below in a series of tables, are discussed in Chapter 3.

1 Numbers and percentages of staff and form tutors

Schools	All Staff	Senior Manag.	Other Staff	Tutors
25	1256	96	1160	763
	100%	7.5%	92.5%	61%*

* Tutors as a % of 'Other Staff' – 66%

2 Numbers and percentages of form tutors on each salary scale

E	D	C/B	Standard Scale
12	63	175	513
1.60%	8.25%	23.0%	67.15%
	32.85%		

3 *Percentages of teachers on each salary scale acting as form tutors*

E	D	C/B	Standard Scale
12/57	63/135	175/291	513/677
21.0%	46.5%	60.0%	75.8%

4 *Salary scales and proportion of staff with each allowance used as form tutors in some individual schools*

School	E	D	C/B	Standard Scale
A	2/4	5/7	10/18	19/26
B	0/3	0/5	5/10	25/28
C	0/0	5/5	4/5	9/15
D	1/2	4/6	4/11	16/23

5 *Distribution of staff as form tutors across the 'Years'*

(Given as average scale points per form in each 'Year', using $E = 4$ points, $D = 3$, $C/B = 2$, Standard Scale $= 1$)

Year	12	11	10	9	8	7
Points	2.7	1.9	1.7	1.5	1.4	1.4

Appendix B

Questionnaires completed by the form tutors in three secondary schools selected by us, on the basis of their Deputies' descriptions, as being in different places on the 'tutor ascendant' to 'tutor subordinate' scale.

Form Tutor Questionnaire (1)

Dear Colleague,

We are presently conducting a small research project into what teachers do as form tutors, what they are expected to do and what they would like to be able to do. We would be extremely grateful if you could spare us the time to fill in the attached questionnaire. You will see that the questions are broken up into groups of three.

Within each group of three statements would you first put a letter 'A' against that statement which most closely represents *your present position* as a form tutor.

Then, within the same group of statements, put a letter 'B' against the one which most closely represents *what you would like your position to be*.

You may believe that one or more of the tasks described by the statements should not be part of a form tutor's job. If you do, instead of putting a 'B' against one statement will you please put a line through the group of three statements about that task.

Thank you for reading so far. We hope that you will be able to help us, but would you return the questionnaire, completed or not, to . . . as soon as possible.

P Griffiths/K Sherman

Form Tutor Questionnaire (1)

1 **Access to confidential information**
a   You feel that you have full access to all information about pupils.
b   Information about pupils is available to you on request.
c   You believe confidential information about pupils is withheld from you.
2 **Involvement in reception and induction of new pupils**
a   You play a central part in the reception and induction of new pupils.
b   You are informed in advance that a new pupil will arrive.
c   New pupils are sent to join your form without prior notification.
3 **Receipt of referrals from subject teachers**
a   Subject teachers contact you in the first instance when worried about a pupil.
b   Subject teachers may keep you in touch with worries about pupils but not regularly or as part of the process.
c   Subject teachers go directly to the pastoral Head in serious cases and you are not necessarily informed.
4 **Initiating contacts with parents**
a   Letters to parents are written by you on your own initiative.
b   You can suggest to the pastoral Head that a letter to parents is required.
c   The pastoral Head will write to parents without necessarily informing you.
5 **Initiating action on absence**
a   You are basically responsible for attendance, calling in help when you feel the need.
b   The pastoral Head follows up absence enquiries initiated by you.
c   You mark the register but take no further action on absence.
6 **Educational and vocational guidance**
a   You play a major part in helping your pupils with vocational and educational decisions.
b   All educational and vocational advice is centralised but you are informed of decisions made.
c   All educational and vocational advice is centralised and you are not involved in these procedures.
7 **Interviews with parents**
a   You interview parents, at home or school, on your own initiative.
b   The decision to interview a parent has to be ratified by the pastoral Head but you are still able to be present to do the interview.
c   You might be told that a parent was about to be interviewed but not necessarily so, and even then you would not normally be present.
8 **Participation in case conferences**
a   You are present at case conferences on members of your form.
b   Your views are solicited before a case conference takes place.

c   You are usually informed that a case conference has been held on a member of your form.

9   Intervention by senior staff

a   Your views are usually solicited by senior staff before a pupil is seen by them.

b   You are informed – reasonably fully – of any action taken by senior staff over children in your form.

c   Action is taken by senior staff about pupils in your form without you being notified.

10 Assumption of primary responsibility

a   You feel that you have the primary responsibility for the pupils in your form.

b   You feel that while the pastoral Head has major responsibility for care of pupils, you have a significant part to play.

c   You feel that you are basically a register checker.

(Based on Marland, 1974)

Form Tutor Questionnaire (1) – Results

Assessment of tutors' perceptions of current and preferred positions (shown in brackets) on continuum of degrees of responsibility for pupils in form (results aggregated since pattern of responses virtually indentical in all three schools).

	Index	*Ascendant* %	*Neutral* %	*Subordinate* %
1	Access to confidential information	19(84)	75(16)	6(0)
2	Involvement in reception and induction of new pupils	3(72)	2(28)	25(0)
3	Receipt of referrals from subject teachers	3(84)	53(13)	44(3)
4	Initial contacts with parents by letter	3(34)	50(63)	47(3)
5	Initiating action on absence	34(63)	60(34)	6(3)
6	Educational and vocational guidance	22(66)	40(31)	38(3)
7	Interviewing parents	3(50)	19(50)	78(0)
8	Participation in case conferences	25(78)	53(22)	22(0)
9	Intervention by senior staff	12(69)	41(31)	47(0)
10	Carer or register clerk	4(56)	4(44)	16(0)

Form Tutor Questionnaire (2)

Dear Colleague,

You will see that this questionnaire is in two parts.

The first part relates the task of being a form tutor to the other tasks which have traditionally been seen as part of a teacher's overall job in a school. The second part lists some of the specific tasks that a school might expect a form tutor, or a subject teacher, or perhaps both, to consider as part of their role.

In Part 1 please consider the tasks listed and select **three** which you think are the most important, and **three** which you think are the least important, marking them with '/' and 'X' respectively.

In Part 2 please consider whether you see each of the tasks listed as a significant part of (A) a form tutor's role, and (B) a subject teacher's role, answering yes or no under (A) and (B) for each question.

Thank you for having read so far. We hope that you will be able to help us but would you return the questionnaire, completed or not, to . . . as soon as possible.

P Griffiths/K Sherman

Form Tutor Questionnaire (2)

Part 1 A Teacher's Tasks (in addition to classroom contact with pupils)

Please mark with '/' those 3 of the following tasks that you see as 'most important' and with 'X', 3 that you see as 'least important'.

Keeping a forecast of work, marking regularly and keeping records of pupils' progress. . . . .

Attending departmental meetings in order to participate in revising work schemes or forming departmental policies, for example, on homework, assessment and so on. . . . .

Keeping up to date with developments in curriculum and teaching techniques by means of reading and attending appropriate courses. . . . .

Being a form tutor. . . . .

Taking part in out-of-school activities. . . . .

Assisting with the smooth running of the school, eg duties, displays, care of fabric etc. . . . .

Consulting and informing parents and co-operating with
appropriate outside agencies. . . . .

Attending staff and other whole-school meetings/assemblies. . . . .

Taking a reasonable share in the school's responsibility for
the classes of colleagues who are unavoidably absent. . . . .

Part 2 A Form Tutor's or a Teacher's Tasks

Do you see each of the following as a significant part of (A) a form tutor's
role and (B) a subject teacher's role? Please answer yes/no for each statement.

	(A)	(B)
To establish a warm relationship with the members of the group, showing sensitivity to their personal needs.	. . . .	. . . .
To encourage members of the group to accept a responsible attitude towards their membership of the school.	. . . .	. . . .
To check uniform and encourage a smart personal appearance and a pride in good standards.	. . . .	. . . .
To record on pupils' personal files all relevant information, keeping these files up to date and ensuring that senior colleagues are aware of changes.	. . . .	. . . .
To encourage good peer relationships and an atmosphere of well-being in the group.	. . . .	. . . .
To take every possible opportunity to become acquainted with the parents of the members the group.	. . . .	. . . .
To monitor and guide the behaviour and work of each pupil as appropriate, with regard to the comments of colleagues on members of the group.	. . . .	. . . .
To ensure that letters to parents are delivered, timetables and other routine administrative matters are dealt with as speedily as possible, and that notices of detentions, medicals and special meetings are passed on in time.	. . . .	. . . .
To complete the termly assessments to parents and, if appropriate, also co-ordinating other teacher's reports and giving a coherent comment on the 'whole pupil'.	. . . .	. . . .

157

To support other staff – checking homework and examination timetables, developing study and revision skills, checking pupils on daily or weekly report and in any other appropriate way.   . . . .

To act as mediator, protecting the well-being and needs of the individual pupil against the demands of the institution.   . . . .

To register the group and follow up absence and lateness, drawing the attention of senior colleagues to pupils whose attendance record gives cause for concern.   . . . .

Form Tutor Questionnaire 2 (Part 1) – Results

	Task	*High* %	*Med* %	*Low* %
1	Keeping a forecast of work, marking regularly and keeping records of pupils' progress.	85	12	3
2	Keeping up to date with developments in curriculum and teaching techniques by means of reading and attending appropriate courses.	69	12	19
3	Attending departmental meetings in order to participate in reviewing work schemes or forming departmental policies on, for example, homework, assessment and so on.	46	46	8
4	Consulting and informing parents and co-operating with appropriate outside agencies.	39	58	3
5	**Being a form tutor**	27	50	23
6	Assisting with the smooth running of the school, eg duties, displays, care of fabric etc.	16	62	23
7	Taking part in out-of-school activities.	15	46	39
8	Attending staff and other whole-school meetings/assemblies.	15	31	54
9	Taking a reasonable share in the school's responsibility for classes of colleagues who are unavoidably absent.	3	12	95

Task	Significant in form tutor's role (%)	Significant in subject teacher's role (%)
To establish a warm relationship with the members of the group, showing sensitivity to their personal needs.	100	100
To encourage members of the group to accept a responsible attitude towards their membership of the school.	100	94
To check uniform and encourage a smart personal appearance and pride in good standards.	94	72
To record on pupils' personal files all relevant information, keeping these files up to date and ensuring that senior colleagues are aware of changes.	91	28
To encourage good peer relationships and an atmosphere of well-being in the group.	100	97
To take every possible opportunity to become acquainted with the parents of the members of the group.	100	87
To monitor and guide the behaviour and work of each pupil as appropriate, with regard to the comments of colleagues on members of the group.	97	78
To ensure that letters to parents are delivered, timetables and other routine administrative matters are dealt with as speedily as possible, and that notices of detentions, medicals, and special meetings are passed on in time.	97	25

Task	Significant in form tutor's role (%)	Significant in subject teacher's role (%)
To complete the termly assessments to parents and, if appropriate, also co-ordinating other teachers' reports and giving a coherent comment on the 'whole pupil'.	97	47
To support other staff – checking homework and examination timetables, developing study and revision skills, checking pupils on daily or weekly report and in any other appropriate way.	94	69
To act as mediator, protecting the well-being and needs of the individual pupil against the demands of the institution.	100	72
To register the group and follow up lateness and absence, drawing the attention of senior colleagues to pupils whose attendance record gives cause for concern.	100	72

Appendix C

Valley School

Role of the Form Tutor

The aims and goals of the pastoral advisory team and the tutor teams are the same as the aims and goals of the school, but within that framework the tutors have quite specific management goals. These are:

1 To manage throughout their time in school each student she/he has in her/his care, to check the progress of individuals, to give help and support where required and to interpret the goals and aims of the school and its policies to students.
2 To act as advocate for the students in all matters relating to school so that the student always has someone to speak for them in any situation which may arise.
3 To oversee the personal, social and moral development of each student in her/his care. To participate as a member of the tutor team in devising a programme aimed at securing personal and social development of students and to implement it within the tutor group.
4 To monitor the attendance, punctuality, behaviour and appearance of each student in the tutor group.
5 To communicate with parents concerning all aspects of student development within the tutor group, and to interpret the goals and aims of the school and its policies to parents.
6 To work with the pastoral adviser for their Year and other tutors in the team, to ensure a consistent and fair approach to rewards and sanctions aimed at securing good relationships.
7 To work and communicate with other staff as necessary for the benefit of the student.
8 To assist and support the pastoral adviser in the maintenance of the team of tutors.

9 To work with such external agencies as may be necessary, in conjunction with the pastoral advisory team.

Role of the Pastoral Adviser

The aims and goals of the pastoral advisory team and the tutor teams are the same as the aims and goals of the school, but within that framework the pastoral advisers have specific management goals. These are:

1 To manage and lead the team of tutors positively and enthusiastically, with the aim of securing the maximum benefit for the students.

2 To enable and facilitate the work of the form tutor, who is primarily responsible for the students in her/his own tutor groups.

3 To interpret the goals and aims of the school and its policies to the tutor team.

4 To lead the team of tutors to develop, deliver and evaluate a programme of personal, social and moral development for the students in the Year group. To supervise the implementation by each tutor of this programme and of a programme of educational and vocational guidance and review.

5 To supervise the maintenance of full and up-to-date records for every student in the Year.

6 To supervise the duty functions of the team of tutors.

7 To be responsible for the organisation and delivery of Year assemblies.

8 To assist and support the Senior Pastoral Adviser in the maintenance of the pastoral advisory team.

9 To seek to establish the understanding of all staff that there are no divisions between the pastoral and academic aspects of a student's school career.

Appendix D

A. Highlands School: The Role of the Form Tutor

Daily and termly routine for Form Tutors

Please note that the following points, which represent a mixture of philosophy and practice, are not in any order of priority. The whole document is intended to be amended periodically following discussion – please raise, at the earliest opportunity, points which are not clear or procedures to which you would like to suggest modifications.

1 Relationships
It is the form teacher's role to establish a relationship with the members of their form based on respect, warmth and acceptance, to encourage good peer relationships and an atmosphere of well-being in the form, and to take a positive interest in the involvement of members of the form in all aspects of their school life – appearance, work, behaviour, extra-curricular activities etc. There are good functional reasons for this, in the sense that the school as an institution and individual tutors need to know how a pupil 'ticks': the context against which they are operating.

It needs to be remembered that the form teacher is likely to be considerably more skilled at developing relationships than the pupils and therefore needs to take the initiative. The objective is for each individual pupil to feel valued and of worth to a significant adult, as well having increased opportunities to experience success.

It is natural for a form teacher to have a sensitive concern for the health and lifestyle of the members of the form and to take an interest in, for example, their hobbies or choice of occupation or training after school. It is necessary to remember, however, that it is a pupil's right not to discuss matters which he or she considers private and outside the concern of the school, and that an individual pupil may be right to resist pressure to live their life or to change in the way that a tutor may feel appropriate.

2 Registers

(i) Please ensure that your register is returned to the reception desk by 9.30am and 1.30pm respectively – Year Heads/tutors/senior staff/ secretaries need to consult them frequently, and their absence can be a major inconvenience.

(ii) Please obtain notes explaining absences as soon as possible after the pupil has returned to school. If no note has been obtained within three days of the start of an absence, please prepare a request letter to be sent home – standardized letters are available in the Year Head's office. Similarly, if there is a single unexplained absence of which you are suspicious, or a regular pattern of half-day or day absences, standard letters are available. (Please inform your Year Head if you plan to use one of these.)

(iii) Please indicate that a note has been received by placing the letter N over the last absence. Please initial and date letters received and place them in the envelopes attached to back cover of register. Absence notes should be filed regularly in individual envelopes which are stored in files in the staffroom. PLEASE DO NOT REMOVE FILES FROM THE STAFFROOM since they may be needed by our Educational Social Worker.

(iv) In circumstances where the normal medical reasons do not apply, the following symbols should be used to indicate reasons for absence:
W   Work Experience
D   Doctor, dentist or hospital appointment
I   Interview
P   Phone call (acceptable in lieu of note)
V   Educational visit/field study etc
O   Absence note sent out
T   Truancy
H   Holiday

(v) If a pupil leaves/transfers to another school or in some other way leaves your register, please rule through the rest of the term and explain the reason (eg left to High Park).

(vi) When a pupil is so late that he/she misses registration, please record this at the next registration by an 'L' over the absence mark, unless this has already been done by the secretaries at the reception desk. Please discuss with your Year Head if a member of your form is regularly or frequently late – they may well be dodging the late book procedure. Half termly checks will be made of attendance and punctuality, and letters will be sent home either warning parents or commending a pupil's attendance or punctuality as appropriate.

(vii) Please note that daily and weekly totals MUST be completed at the bottom of each week's column, but the individual totals at the side and the calculation of percentages are not required.

(viii) Please remove ALL unwanted or outdated materials from registers weekly, if not daily. Please remember that registers are legal documents consulted by ESW's, Social Workers etc, and do not always reflect well on our professionalism. Unnecessary clutter in registers also leads, too frequently, to important messages to both staff and pupils being missed until too late.

(ix) Please bring any unusual patterns of lateness or absence (particularly prolonged absence) to the attention of your appropriate Year Head. Year Heads are expected to check registers once a week, and discuss with you or ask for follow-up on any points which they note. No system, however, is infallible and even the most obvious discrepancies can be missed until embarrassing questions start being asked.

(x) Please do not leave blanks in your register. A pupil must be marked present or absent at each registration.

3 Absence/records

(i) Please note points in 2 above.

(ii) Where there is a reason to suspect that an absence is in some way suspect, or requires following up, then reference should be made to our ESW who is usually in school immediately after break each day of the week. Please observe the following procedure:

A Pupil's Absence Record should be made up for each pupil in your class who has been absent. These MUST be stored in the rack in the Staffroom and made up-to-date weekly. Please record absences only, whether a note or reply to request letter has been received and (in summary) the reason for absence. Records that you wish followed up should be placed in the ESW return slot – please check the ESW return slot regularly for responses. The ESW should discuss all referrals with you or your Year Head **before** a visit is made.

4 Lates

(i) Please note points in 2 above.

(ii) Pupils arriving late must report to registration, or the reception desk if registration is over – where their lateness will be entered on a slip which should then be placed in your register – or to the Dining Room, on assembly mornings.

(iii) ALL pupils who are late should be requested to report to the Year Head at 3.30pm to explain their lateness. Please inform your Form of this and stress that it is not in lieu of other punishment but will be taken into account. If a pupil has not attended to explain their lateness, then no concessions will be made in terms of detention (see below).

(iv) After a pupil has been unacceptably late three times during the course of a term, they will be placed in detention by the Year Head. They will be informed of this via the register on the preceding day by a *pink* form. Failure to attend will incur more severe punishment.

5 Year detentions
(i) Please note points in 4 above.
(ii) Although primarily intended as a lates detention, the weekly Year detention is available to any form teacher (or subject teacher – though problems occurring within lessons should normally be referred first to the appropriate Head of Subject or Team Leader) who has had reason to punish a pupil by their own detention and has not been satisfied with the pupil's attendance, attitude or work in that detention, or who feels that an incident warrants a more severe formal punishment.

Please discuss such cases with the Year Head and with the appropriate Team Leader. Staff who place pupils in Year detention are normally expected to provide appropriate work.

6 Pupils causing concern
Form teachers should take note of the comments of colleagues on members of the form and should be the first in line of action in helping each pupil to cope with his/her difficulties, or to rectify difficulties they are creating for others. Sometimes this will demand a disciplinary response; at others the offering of a listening ear or helping hand, or the sharing of ideas and experience, or the referring of the problem on to the Year Head or Counsellor (see later). The balance between discipline and support can be the most difficult problem the form tutor has to face.

Where a form teacher feels cause for disciplinary concern exists over behaviour, attitude, work across several subjects etc, such concern should be brought to the attention of the Year Head/Team leader. Information will then be gathered by a *green* form from all staff dealing with that pupil, and on the basis of that information one or more of the following courses of action will be initiated:

(i) Discussion with Year Head.
(ii) Daily report for a few days.
(iii) Weekly report with copy sent to parents, who will be invited to discuss contents.
(iv) Request for parents to attend school as a matter of urgency.
(v) Placement of pupil under constant supervision for a limited period of time.

It is legitimate for the form teacher's role in all of this to be that of an advocate, protecting the well-being and needs of the individual member of the form – explaining and humanising the school's organisation, the demands of staff (academic, pastoral and ancillary) and the rules and code of behaviour of the school. This may even require the direct intercession of the form teacher as a protestor on the part of an individual pupil. Certainly, if a pupil is facing serious disciplinary action the form teacher should feel able to speak on his or her behalf wherever possible.

7 Reports to parents

These are an important – sometimes our only – channel of communication with parents. In their comments, therefore, tutors should remember to address the parents and not the child (words of advice to a pupil can still be included of course, but in the form 'Joanne must remember to' etc). Tutors should try to make comments positive and constructive, wherever possible offering suggestions as to how a pupil might overcome a problem or achieve an objective, rather than just stating that they exist. A poor conduct assessment, for example, could well be amplified in the written comment, or put into an appropriate contact. Tutors should avoid just writing a summary of what is already obvious from the subject comments. In fact, a tutor should be able to greatly add to the overall report in terms of

- personal development and maturity
- positions of responsibility accepted (and measure of success in fulfilling them)
- contributions towards school or form efforts in competitive events, fund raising activities, social events etc
- contributions towards Personal Development Programme
- attitudes towards authority, dress, code of conduct
- relationships with peers and teachers
- vocational aspirations and their apparent appropriateness

Tutors should remember not to be too pedantic in their comments, not making firm statements unless they can be backed up and never making categorical predictions of any sort – always adding a qualification like 'should, provided etc . . .'. Tutors should remember also that school is a closed book to many of our parents, perhaps because things have changed so much since they were at school; perhaps because they were unsuccessful and still harbour resentment; perhaps because they don't really talk to their children about school. The Report or Grade Sheet should be the opening comments in a dialogue, and should therefore present an invitation to the parents to come in and participate in their child's education.

Reports are only one means of communicating with parents – and a limited one in that they are formal and happen only at well-spaced fixed points in the school year. More frequent contact can be made through letters, phone calls, home visits by our Educational Social Worker or, where a form teacher feels confident in doing so, a personal home visit. Form teachers are free to initiate any of these but it is always wise to inform the Year Head or to record the fact in the Day Book (see later), since it is not unknown for other contacts (eg by subject teachers) to have been initiated prior to internal consultation having taken place.

Although all of the above methods of communication can be used to discuss with parents difficulties which their child might be experiencing they are much more useful and *positive* if they are used to pass on a compliment, to let parents know how pleased we are with something that their child has done. As a basic minimum a form teacher should aim to have at least one such positive contact with the parents of each pupil in his/her form during the course of a year – in school during a parents evening, for example, or by home visit in person, by phone or by letter.

8 References/court reports

We receive frequent requests from Colleges, Employers, the Courts, Social Services, etc for information on our pupils. Normally these will be drafted by either a Year Head or a Deputy on behalf of the Principal – but only after the tutor has been consulted. On occasions, information has to be given over the phone or at very short notice and consultation may not be possible. Under normal circumstances, however, form teachers will receive a questionnaire on which they are asked to note, *in as much detail as possible*, information which can then be incorporated into the report. Tutors should remember that even the most obvious of points can get missed – a tutor is probably in a far better position than a Year Head to know the real pupil, certainly for the 60% of pupils who fall ino the 'grey zone'. We owe it to our pupils and to our own professionalism to present the best and most accurate picture of them that we can. If time is pressing, tutors can make comments verbally, so that the Year Head has at least some information to work on.

9 Communication

(i) *Day Book*

Each Years' Day Book – a large diary – is one of the means by which the members of a pastoral team liaise. It is intended to communicate and record incidents which occur on a day-by-day basis. It *should not* be removed – except to read of course – from the Year Head's desk or pigeon hole and is available to all members of the team to read and to add information to.

(ii) *Year Team Meetings*

These will take place at 3.45pm on Tuesday, as notified in the Year Plan. Their function will include the sharing of information and experience on PDP but from time to time they may also be used for the review of procedures, the discussion of a common approach to difficulties and, for example, ways of handling deviations from the published Code of Conduct by individual pupils.

Urgent Notices

Tutors should refer regularly to the 'Pastoral – Urgent' board in the Staffroom, where the names of pupils on whom information is available will be listed; they can then consult the appropriate member of staff.

10 Code of behaviour/uniform regulations

The primary concerns of our pastoral system are the personal development of each pupil, the integration of each pupil into the social framework of the community of the school, and the establishment of an ethos and environment within which effective learning can take place.

The published code of behaviour and other rules and regulations are means to those ends and not ends in themselves. Pupils must know in detail that they exist and that they will be enforced quietly but firmly. They must see that the staff will lead by example and also be governed by the dictum of being courteous and considerate at all times. They must also be aware, in addition, that the school will be sympathetic to an individual pupil or family's problems in its interpretation and enforcement of the Code and Regulations.

The current Code of Behaviour and Dress Code are as follows.

Pupils at this school are expected to conform to the following code of behaviour – sympathetically and sensibly, but firmly, enforced.

1 PUPILS SHOULD WAIT QUIETLY OUTSIDE TEACHING ROOMS OR AREAS BEFORE THE START OF THE LESSONS. They should not enter until supervised by a member of staff and should then move to their places quietly and sensibly. Younger classes in particular should remain standing until told to sit, at which point a register of the class will be taken.

2 PUPILS SHOULD MAKE THEIR WAY IN AN ORDERED MANNER FROM LESSON TO LESSON, SO ARRIVING PUNCTUALLY. To this end Staff make every effort to release pupils promptly at the end of lessons. Pupils unreasonably late for lessons should expect to make up the time wasted.

3 PUPILS SHOULD REMOVE IN LESSONS AND BETWEEN LESSONS ALL OUTDOOR COATS, HATS, GLOVES ETC. Bags should be kept off desk/table tops and should be tucked neatly under, or by, their chairs/seats.

4 PUPILS SHOULD NOT LEAVE A CLASSROOM AT THE END OF A LESSON UNTIL THEY ARE TOLD TO DO SO. It should be noted that the bell system is merely a warning to staff. Pupils should, when told to do so, stand, put their chairs under desks/tables and wait quietly. When released they should leave the room quietly and in an orderly manner.

5 PUPILS SHOULD LEAVE TEACHING ROOMS OR AREAS IN A TIDY STATE. Any rubbish or scrap paper on, under or around the desks/tables should be placed in the bin before the class leaves the room.

6 PUPILS SHOULD DISPLAY TOWARDS STAFF AND TOWARDS ONE ANOTHER THE SAME GOOD MANNERS AND COURTESY THAT STAFF ARE EXPECTED TO SHOW TOWARDS THEM. Doors should be held open for others, conversations should not be interrupted without an apology or polite request, unruly behaviour should be discouraged, oral lessons should be conducted in an ordered, disciplined manner and so on.

7 PUPILS SHOULD EXPECT TO PROVIDE THEIR OWN WRITING INSTRUMENTS, INCLUDING PENS, PENCILS AND RULER. In addition, where appropriate, (especially in the Upper School) they should provide their own simple geometry set, electronic calculator, dictionary and atlas.

8 PUPILS SHOULD DEVELOP A PRIDE IN THE APPEARANCE OF THEIR WORK. All written work should be neat and tidy, completed in ink, with proper titles and dates underlined.

9 PUPILS SHOULD EXPECT TO RECEIVE HOMEWORK APPROPRIATE TO THE WORK THEY ARE DOING. These are best recorded in Homework Diaries which can be signed by parents at regular intervals, and should be periodically examined by form teachers. Homework should be completed and handed in on time.

School dress code

The regulations most likely to cause difficulties to a form teacher are those concerning uniform, earrings or hairstyle. Deviations must be questioned and, if appropriate, dealt with firmly. Persistent offenders – or offenders immediately following a warning – should be sent to the Year Head or to the deputy Head who will, if appropriate after investigation of individual circumstances, send the pupil home. It must be remembered however, that a pupil who is excluded from school for whatever reason, is both missing education in the short term, and unlikely to be totally co-operative in the long term. The only pupils who should be showing any deviation from the regulations will be those with written permission to do so, and those will be as few as possible.

The current regulations, as they appear in the information booklet issued to intake parents, are as follows:

Dress Code for both boys and girls:

Plain dark grey or black skirt or trousers
Plain white shirt or shirt blouse with sleeves
Plain maroon tie
Plain maroon V-necked pullover or collarless cardigan

Plain black, grey or white socks or beige tights
Sensible and appropriate footwear.

Any make-up or jewellery worn should be simple and discreet and it must again be borne in mind that in some classes jewellery will have to be removed or taped over for safety reasons – this is particularly so in craft workshops and in Physical Education lessons.

11 Assemblies
Since we do not have a space in which we can assemble the whole school, assemblies take place in the Hall as follows:

Monday	Year 8 (Senior Teacher/Year Head)
Tuesday	Year 10 (Senior Teacher/Year Head)
Wednesday	Year 9 (Senior Teacher/Year Head)
Thursday	Year 11 (Senior Teacher/Year Head)
Friday	Alternately, forms 1–3 or 4–6 from all Year groups (Principal or Deputy/Senior Teacher)

Form teachers are expected to accompany their form to assembly, registering them in the Hall on assembly days, sitting with them and seeing them out at the end.

Any member of staff may be excused from assembly itself on religious grounds, but a form tutor so doing would be expected to assist with the arrival, registration, settling and dismissal of his/her form.

Tutors who feel able to contribute to the assembly rota will find their contributions warmly received. A rota exists for forms to set out and clear away the chairs in the Hall for assemblies – tutors need to ensure that their forms are aware of this.

12 Sharing responsibility
Form teachers need to encourage members of their form to accept greater responsibility in, and a more responsible attitude towards, their membership of the school and of society in general. There are a number of established vehicles for this, though others could be created through form teacher–pupil negotiation:

(i)   Year groups are encouraged to undertake some special effort for charity or to become more actively involved in the local community – individual groups of pupils have, for example, in the past developed contacts with special schools, nurseries and old peoples' homes.

(ii) At Christmas, Year groups have regularly prepared Christmas Hampers which, together with Christmas cards designed by individual pupils and printed in school, have been distributed to senior citizens in the local area.

171

(iii)　Forms need to elect representatives to both Year and School councils who will need to consult the form prior to meetings and to feed back, not only formal minutes, but the details of discussions. In the case of the School council the Parent Teacher Association have agreed to make £100 available each year, which the council can spend on projects of its own choosing.

(iv)　As noted before, forms share responsibility for putting out and clearing chairs for assemblies. Individual Year groups are also asked to assist in the running of the school as follows (tutors need to be aware of the respective rotas and to see that they are filled and that absentees are covered).

L form　Runners for internal and external exams and medical inspections

M form　Receptionists in Main foyer

U form　Librarians

S form　Stewards

13 Personal development programme (PDP)

This programme – scheduling for the year attached – provides a vehicle for the delivery of our Social Education Programme (which makes a significant contribution to the Cross Curricular Themes aspect of National Curriculum) and for Tutor Review and Guidance.

As can be seen from the schedule the programme is broken up into six-week blocks. An individual tutor will spend six weeks with his or her form (led and supported by a Year Head) working on a series of 'getting to know you' groupwork exercises from one of the programme themes, followed by six weeks withdrawing individual members of the form for Review and Guidance interviews, while the remainder of the form are taken by one of two support teams of staff who will be working with them on further aspects of the same four themes – Myself and Others, Study, Our Community, and Jobs and Work.

14 Review and Guidance and Records of Achievement

Form Tutor Review and Guidance is based on a proforma, on which pupils ask individual subject teachers to comment on their work and on which they and their parents are also encouraged to comment. Tutors need to give out the proformas approximately one week in advance of appointments and then to encourage their completion. During the course of the Review and Guidance interview it is anticipated that form tutor and pupil together will decide on one or more targets for improvement or consolidation over the following 6–12 week period. Monitoring of progress towards those targets is the pupil's responsibility but they will obviously need encouragement and support to do so.

Completed proformas are stored in form rooms in each individual pupil's 'Achievement File', which is also used to store the regular comments on, and summaries of activities and experiences that the pupils make during and at the end of each year. In the January of Year 11 each pupil uses the accumulated material in their 'Achievement' file to compile the 'Personal Statement' and the 'Interests, experiences and achievements' pages in the summative 'Record of Achievement'. Tutors may need to encourage and support individual pupils in this but the final statements are the pupil's property and need to express their own ideas and feelings in their own words. Tutors, however, will need to more directly influence what is included in the third 'Curriculum Statement' page of the RoA. More detailed guidance is available at the appropriate time.

15 Compact

Highlands School is very firmly part of the Dudley Compact and our pupils in Years 10 and 11 are therefore working towards compact goals in terms of

- Attendance
- Punctuality
- Completion of coursework
- Work experience
- Personal development.

Form tutors will need to be actively involved in monitoring the progress of individual members of their form, using standard proformas. Attendance and punctuality percentages are, of course, calculated from the register; data on completion of coursework, however, will need to be obtained from individual subject teachers.

16 Counselling

For approximately one third of each week we have the services of a member of the Dudley Educational Counselling Service. This is a centrally-based service, staffed by trained and experienced counsellors who are independent of the school but offer a counselling service to our pupils.

If a form tutor becomes concerned or worried about any pupil then he or she can suggest to their Year Head that the pupils are referred to the counsellor. When the referral has been agreed by all concerned – pupil, parents and school – then a series of weekly meetings can be offered in which the pupil can talk privately and confidentially about any difficulties or worries they may have in any aspect of their life.

Permission for referral must always be obtained from the parents and the counsellor will usually contact the parents at some point in the process of counselling. Equally, tutors should expect to have regular contact with our counsellor if one of their tutees is being counselled.

17 Pupil records

All pupils have (centrally stored in the admin. office) a 'yellow peril' school record file. Tutors need to keep all filing of letters to parents, report copies, interview notes etc up to date. Tutors also need to remember that these are public records and that parents have a right to see what is recorded in them. All comments need, therefore, to reflect the very best of our professionalism.

B. Highlands School: Looking After Your Child (Extracted from *Information for Parents 1990/91*)

Among the compliments that we are always most pleased to hear are that we are an 'especially caring school', that our pupils are 'particularly open and friendly' and that relationships between our staff and pupils are 'excellent'. We encourage every pupil to do the best that they can and, if at all possible, to discover success in some area. In addition, however, we try to make it clear to them that what they are and what they do is just as important to us. The entire staff are involved in this part of our work but the focus of our caring is on our Form Tutors, who are directly responsible for the progress and welfare of each member of their form; and our Heads of Year, who lead the teams of form tutors within each Year. Should you wish to discuss any aspect of your child's progress or welfare, we would be very happy for you to arrange an appointment with their tutor or, if they are not available, with the Year Head.

The form tutor is responsible for the pupil's well-being on a day-to-day basis. The tutor sees the form twice every day for registration and the Year 8 team in particular see their form for at least one lesson a week, in addition to the Personal Development session on Wednesday mornings. During that session a whole range of different activities can take place but in particular pupils will be encouraged to build up the personal file of achievements and experiences which they will keep throughout their time at school. On three occasions during the year the form tutor will use that time to see individual pupils from the form to discuss with them their own work and development. This procedure, which we call *Review and Guidance*, gives an opportunity for any problems to be resolved and for plans to be made, and for the tutor and pupil to get to know one another on a more individual basis.

In addition to their caring role, form tutors also deal with various aspects of behaviour and of school organisation and administration concerning our pupils.

Sharing responsibility

Our pupils are encouraged to take part in all aspects of school life. Each form elects representatives to meet regularly as a Year Council to put forward ideas raised by their form. Each form also elects a representative to

PERSONAL DEVELOPMENT PROGRAMME   HIGHLANDS SCHOOL & COMMUNITY COLLEGE — DRAFT YEAR PLAN 1989/90
TUTOR REVIEW AND GUIDANCE

FORM TUTORS – NEW YEAR ADMINISTRATION → FORM TUTORS – END OF YEAR ADMINISTRATION (INCLUDES ACTIVITIES WEEK) — Weeks 38-40, 4/7/90-18/7/90 inc.

	Weeks 2-7 13/9/89-18/10/89 inc	Weeks 8-13 1/11/89-6/12/89 inc	Weeks 14-19 13/12/89-24/1/90 inc	Weeks 20-25 31/1/90-14/3/90 inc	Weeks 26-31 21/3/90-9/5/90 inc	Weeks 32-37 16/5/90-27/6/90 inc
L FORM	FORMS WITH TUTORS: **INDUCTION PROGRAMME** (eds)	SUPPORT TEAM: My, P, Mgn, Dn, Ht, Pge, (Eds) — **LEARNING SKILLS** — TUTORS: R&G based on PROFORMA - lead into settling in letter (grades) to Parents	FORMS WITH TUTORS: **MYSELF** (Eds)	SUPPORT TEAM: Sn, My, Mgn, Ru, Wms, (Eds) — **HEALTH/HYGIENE & FIRST AID** — TUTORS: R&G based on Proforma → Action Plan	FORMS WITH TUTORS: **OTHER PEOPLE ARE DIFFERENT** (Eds)	SUPPORT TEAM: Mgn, My, Dn, P, Dn, Pkr (Eds) — **PEOPLE & COMMUNITY** — TUTORS: R&G based on Proformas - lead into Reports to Parents
M FORM	SUPPORT TEAM Dn, An, My, P, Mgn, Pge (On) — **AUTHORITY** — TUTORS: R & G based on Summer Report (L form) - How to improve/overcome identified problems → Action Plan	FORMS WITH TUTORS: **RELATIONSHIPS** (On)	SUPPORT TEAM: Dn, Dh, My, Mgn, Pge, Wms, (On) — **STUDY SKILLS/ CURRICULUM INFO.** — TUTORS: R&G based on Proforma - lead into Report to Parents & eventual options	FORMS WITH TUTORS: **DECISION MAKING & OPTIONS** (On)	SUPPORT TEAM: Cr + full team as required (on) — **JOBS AND WORK** — TUTORS: R&G based on Proformas	FORMS WITH TUTORS: **HEALTH & LEISURE** (On)
U FORM	FORMS WITH TUTORS: **STUDY SKILLS** (By)	SUPPORT TEAM: An, Sn, Dn, Pkr, Wms, (By) — **RELATIONSHIPS AND PARENTHOOD** — TUTORS: R&G based on PROFORMA - lead into settling in grade letters to Parents	FORMS WITH TUTORS: **HEALTH/ABUSE** (By)	SUPPORT TEAM: Dn, An, Dh, P, Ht, Pge, (By) — **VALUES FOR LIFE** (RE) — TUTORS: R&G based on Proformas → Action Plan	FORMS WITH TUTORS: **LAW AND ORDER** (By)	SUPPORT TEAM: Cr, An, Sn, Ht, Pge, (By) — **CAREERS** — TUTORS: R&G based on Proformas - lead into Reports to Parents.
S FORM	SUPPORT TEAM: Rn, Dn, Sn, Ht, Pkr, Wms, (Cpr) — **EXAM/REVISION SKILLS** (Cpr) — TUTORS: R & G based on Summer Report (U form) → Action Plan	FORMS WITH TUTORS: **CAREERS** (Interview skills etc) (Cpr) (Cr)	SUPPORT TEAM: P, Sn, Ht, Rn, An, Pkr, (Cpr.) — **RIGHTS & RESPONSIBILITIES** — TUTORS: R&G based on Proforma & lead into Mock Exam based grade letter to Parents & ROA Summative Document (Simplified form)	FORMS WITH TUTORS: **VALUES FOR LIFE** (RE) (Cpr)	FORMS WITH TUTORS: 1. Modifications to RoA 2. Completion of Work Experience etc. 3. Individual guidance References etc. 4. Private study / Revision	↑ Week 33

Cr: WORK EXPERIENCE – BRIEFING / DEBRIEFING ETC + CAREERS INTERVIEWS – FORM BY FORM.

a whole School Council who meet with the Principal and the senior pupils to raise issues of concern to pupils across all Year groups. Senior pupils are selected each year by both staff and pupils from the members of Year 11 and help us in a number of ways with the running of the school, particularly by helping to organise all of the Year 11 pupils who volunteer to be Stewards (Prefects). Lower down the school, pupils get used to accepting responsibility by acting as runners for exams, taking turns as Receptionists and helping to run the Library.

Absences from school

It is the responsibility of every parent or guardian to ensure that their child attends school every time it is open. It is equally the school's responsibility to know that its pupils are present in school or, if not, the reason why.

If a child is unable to attend school, the following procedures help us both to fulfil those responsibilities.

a   If your child is away please telephone the school or send a note giving an explanation. If a telephone call is made initially, then a note should be brought when the child returns to school confirming the reason. If no message is received after three days then we will write to you and this may be followed up by a visit from our Education Social Worker.

b   If a pupil is having treatment from a doctor or a dentist and needs time out from school, please let their form teacher know in writing before the appointment.

c   If your annual holiday does not coincide with the school holiday then please obtain a holiday form from the school secretary, complete it and return it to their form teacher. Please remember that legally this can only be for two weeks in any one year.

Accidents, illness and other problems

Should your child have an accident at school, he/she will receive first aid and hospital treatment will be obtained if required; similarly, if your child is taken ill he/she will be looked after until such time as he/she can safely be sent home. The school has the facilities to deal with such routine medical problems, but a telephone number for a parent or relative is essential so that you can be contacted if necessary.

As part of the National Health Service screening of all school age children our School Nurse Mrs (...), who is based at (...) Health Centre, and her colleagues have traditionally seen various year groups to conduct hair, teeth and eyesight examinations and to administer BCG and Rubella vaccinations. This year she will again be conducting 'Health Care Interviews' designed to promote the health and well-being of our Year 8 pupils so that hopefully they can reach their full potential without being disadvantaged by ill health. The following aspects of health will be included in the interviews – vision, height, weight and oral hygiene checks.

Reports and Parents' evenings

During a pupil's four years in the school you will receive a report on their progress and work every other term. Some of these will be in the form of a letter showing grades for effort. Some will be longer and more detailed indicating, for example, where more effort might be needed in a particular subject. Following these detailed reports you will be invited to meet with staff to discuss your child's progress and any concerns that they may have. You can, of course, contact the form tutor or subject teachers at any other time in the year to discuss matters of concern. It is important that our pupils see their parents and their teachers working together in their best interests.

You should expect to receive reports as follows:

Year 8 – letter report **December**, full report **July**
Year 9 – full report **February**
Year 10 – letter report **December**, full report **June**
Year 11 – letter report linked to exam entry **January**

Behaviour, work and encouragement

As a school we seek to create a friendly but firm framework in which all pupils can feel happy and secure, and in which they can learn in a proper work-orientated atmosphere. We have a code of behaviour within school which is kept as simple as possible but which is designed to encourage pupils to exercise good manners, consideration to others and common sense. Most occasions where this does not happen are handled immediately within the classroom or corridor but there are times when a more formal punishment is necessary.

On such occasions extra written work may be set for completion at home or a pupil may be detained at the end of the school day (after at least 24 hours notice): you should, of course, expect to be told about this. In serious cases of ill-discipline a senior member of staff may place a pupil on daily or weekly report: you would again be told if such action were necessary. From time to time parents may be asked to come into school to discuss, with a form tutor or with a senior member of staff, their child's behaviour should this continue to be unsatisfactory. Equally, however, you could ask to come in and see those same people if you are concerned about what seems to be happening.

177

Finally, if it becomes necessary a pupil may be excluded from school for a short period of time for continued failure to conform to the code of behaviour. Complete withdrawal from the school, which has to be recommended by the Principal and ratified by the School Governors, is reserved for extremely serious cases, is very rarely used, and only happens when every other avenue to get the pupil to behave and work in a reasonable way has been tried.

The development of discipline, particularly self-discipline, requires more than just punishments, however; it also requires encouragement and support and this positive aspect is, we believe, the more important of the two. We therefore have a system where Merit Certificates are given to pupils who achieve good work in individual classes. There is also a yearly system of progress reviews in which all of the subjects taken by a pupil are considered, with pupils receiving special praise in a number of areas being presented with a School Commendation Certificate. These are, of course, in addition to the reports mentioned previously and to the day-by-day praise and encouragement that form tutors, subject teachers and parents will give them.

Counselling

For one third of each week we have the services of a counsellor from the Educational Counselling Service. This is a centrally-based service, staffed by trained and qualified counsellors who are independent of school and who offer a skilled counselling service to our pupils.

When a Form Tutor becomes concerned or worried about any pupil they can suggest that the pupil is referred to the counsellor. When the referral is agreed by all concerned – pupil, parents and the school – then he can offer a series of weekly meetings in which that pupil can talk privately and confidentially about any difficulties or worries they may have in any aspect of their life. Permission for referral to the counsellor will always be obtained from parents, and he will usually contact the parents, and be happy to talk with them, at some point in the process of counselling.

Should you yourself be worried about your child, and feel that a counsellor could help, we suggest you make contact through their form tutor or Head of Year.

References

Adams, S. 1986: In-Service Training for Tutoring. *Pastoral Care in Education*, 4(1).

Baldwin, J. and Smith, A. 1979/80/81: *Active Tutorial Work* Books 1–5. Basil Blackwell.

Barnes, D. 1976: *From Communication to Curriculum*. Penguin.

Baumrind, D. 1971: Current Patterns of Parental Authority. *Developmental Psychology Monograph*, 4(1) Pt.2, pp1–103. Quoted in Herbert, M. 1987.

Bell, P. and Best, R. 1986: *Supportive Education*. Basil Blackwell.

Best, R., Ribbins, P. and Jarvis, C. 1983: *Education and Care*. Heinemann.

Biddick School Washington, Tyne and Wear: Where Teachers are Learners. *TES*, 4 April 1986.

Blackburn, K. 1975: *The Tutor*. Heinemann.

Blackburn, K. 1983: *Head of House, Head of Year*. Heinemann Educational Books.

Bloomer, M. 1985: *Pastoral Care in a Comprehensive School*. Unpublished Ph.D thesis, University of Exeter.

Burns, R. 1982: *Self-Concept Development and Education*. Holt, Rinehart and Winston.

Coopersmith, S. 1967: *The Antecedents of Self-Esteem*. San Francisco Freeman.

Davies, D. 1976: Schools as Organisations. *Management in Organisations Course Materials*. Open University Press.

Department of Education and Science (DES), 1987: *School Teacher's Pay and Conditions of Employment Proposals*. HMSO 1987.

Dunham, J. 1987: Caring for the Pastoral Carers. *Pastoral Care in Education*, 3(2).

Egan, G. 1975: *The Skilled Helper*. Brooks/Cole Pub. Co. USA.

Ellenby, S. 1985: Ask the Clients! *Pastoral Care in Education*, 3(2) June 1985.

Elton Report, 1989: *Discipline in Schools*. HMSO 1989.

Ericson, E.H. 1965: *Childhood and Society*. Penguin.

Freeman, A. 1987: Pastoral Care and Teacher Stress. *Pastoral Care in Education*, 5(1) February 1987.

Goffman, I. 1968: *Asylums*. Penguin.

Hamblin, D.H. 1978: *The Teacher and Pastoral Care*. Basil Blackwell.

Hamblin, D.H. 1984: *Pastoral Care – a training manual*. Basil Blackwell.

Hanko, G. 1985: *Special Needs in Ordinary Classrooms*. Basil Blackwell.

Harris, R. 1987: Special Relationships. *TES*, 24 July.

Herbert, M. 1987: *Conduct Disorders in Childhood and Adolescence*. John Wiley and Sons.

Her Majesty's Inspectorate (HMI) 1979: *Aspects of Secondary Education in England*. HMSO.

HMI 1989: *Pastoral Care in Secondary Schools. An Inspection of Some Aspects of Pastoral Care in 1987–88*. DES 1989.

Hopson, B. and Scally, M. 1979: *Lifeskills Teaching Programmes*. Lifeskills Associates UK.

Jones, A. 1977: *Counselling Adolescents in Schools*. Kogan Page.

Kitteringham, J. 1987: Pupil's perceptions of the role of the form tutor. *Pastoral Care in Education*, 5(3) November 1987.

Knowle High School, Blackpool: Outstanding Achievement. *TES*, 3 February 1989.

Laing, R.D. 1971: *Knots*. Penguin.

Lang, P. 1983: How Pupils See It: Looking at how pupils perceive pastoral care. *Pastoral Care in Education*, 1(3) November 1983.

Laslett, R., Review of Disruptive Children: Disruptive Schools? by Lawrence, J., Steed, D. and Young, P. 1984: *Pastoral Care in Education*, 3(3) November 1985.

Lawley, P. 1985: The Pastoral Care of Teachers. *Pastoral Care in Education*, 3(3) November 1985.

Lord, E. HMI 1983: Pastoral Care in Education: Principles and Practice. *Pastoral Care in Education*, 1(1) February 1983.

Marland, M. 1974: *Pastoral Care*. Heinemann.

Myers, G. Director, The Training Network, 125 Lazy Hill, Kings Norton, Birmingham B38 9PB.

NAPCE/SCDC 1989: *Whole Person: whole school*. Longman.

Preedy, M. 1981: Managing the Curriculum and Pastoral Care. *Management in the Schools Course Papers*. Open University Press.

Schools Council Health Education Project 13–18 1980: Self-Concept and Self-Esteem. *Co-ordinator's Guide*. Southampton University.

Shaw, M.: *Survival Manual For Form Tutors*. Oxfordshire LEA.

Silcox, A. Staff Development and the Problems of Teachers. In Hamblin, D.H. 1981: *Problems and Practice of Pastoral Care*. Basil Blackwell.

Staub, E. 1975: *The Development of Prosocial Behaviour in Children*. General Learning Press, Morrison, New Jersey. Quoted in Herbert, M. 1987.

Stibbs, J. 1987: Staff Care and Development. *Pastoral Care in Education*, 5(1) February 1987.

Richardson, E. 1973: *The Teacher, the School and the Task of Management*. Heinemann.

Tattum, D. 1984: Pastoral Care and Disruptive Pupils. *Pastoral Care in Education*, 2(1) February 1984.

Tattum, D. 1982: *Disruptive Pupils in Schools and Units*. John Wiley and Son.

The Peers School, Oxford: *The School Book*.

TES, 17 March 1989 pA9: Article on the Elton Report.

The Teacher 1990: The Stress Factor, Vol 1 Spring Term 1990.

Williams, T. and Williams, N. 1980: 'Personal and Social Development in the School Curriculum' in Schools Council Health Education Project 13–18. *Co-ordinator's Guide*. Southampton University.

Williamson, D. 1980: 'Pastoral Care: or pastoralization' in Best, R., Jarvis, C. and Ribbins, P. (eds), *Perspectives on Pastoral Care*. Heinemann Educational Books.